D0559466

The Bathroom Joke Book

By

Russ "The Flush" Edwards

RED-LETTER PRESS, INC.
SADDLE RIVER, NEW JERSEY

Introduction

"It's hard to be funny and clean."
—Mae West

Funny and Clean — that was exactly the task assigned to Russ "The Flush" Edwards for *The Bathroom Joke Book*. Four years later, if not a squeaky clean version of jokes, one-liners, and witticisms, the material he's produced has been "sanitized for your protection."

Given the glut of tasteless humor on the market, *The Bathroom Joke Book* will bring a breath of fresh air to your bathroom.

If there's any one joke that offends any one person in this book it is unintended. All of the humor is meant in fun, not to poke fun.

As a matter of fact, as you'll find when you read on, the author has made sure to target some of his more pointed material at jokebook publishers themselves.

And, as a matter of fact, that is why this jokebook publisher has a message to the author about royalty payments: Russ, see the last punch line in this book.

Yours flushingly,

Jack Kreismer
Publisher

Figuring she had a few minutes to run errands before the plumber arrived, a woman slipped out but as luck would have it, just a moment later the plumber showed up and knocked on the door.

"Who is it?" the lady's pet parrot piped up, the only phrase, by the way, that the bird had ever learned.

"It's the plumber," came the cordial reply.

"Who is it?"

"It's the plumber!" answered the plumber a bit louder.

"Who is it?" repeated the parrot.

"It's the plumber!!" the man shouted.

"Who is it?"

"IT'S the @#$%&! PLUMBER!" the tradesman screamed at the top of his lungs while jumping up and down in frustration on the porch. Suddenly, he had a massive heart attack and collapsed in front of the door.

Just then the woman returned home and seeing the crumpled body on her porch exclaimed, "Heavens! Who is it?"

And the parrot chimed in with, "It's the plumber!"

* * * *

Deep in the darkest jungle on the sub-continent, a lost and unarmed British explorer stumbled into a clearing and found himself face to face with an 800 pound Bengal tiger. Immediately the explorer dropped to his knees in desperate prayer. After a minute or so he happened to catch sight of the tiger right alongside him, on his knees with paws raised in supplication. Surprised, the explorer said, "Now see here, I am on my knees praying to my Lord for deliverance. You're only a dumb animal, what could you possibly be doing?"

And the tiger says, "Whatdaya think, bud? I'm saying grace!"

Thoughts from the Throne

"Please accept my resignation. I don't care to belong to any club that will have me as a member."
—Groucho Marx

While driving along the back roads of Maine, a city slicker caught sight of a three-legged chicken running just alongside of his car.

Glancing at the speedometer, he noted that he was going 40 miles per hour. The city feller decided to see just how fast that chicken could go so he sped up to 60. The chicken kept pace.

Feeling like the frustrated coyote in the "Roadrunner" cartoons, he pushed the accelerator down and shifted into overdrive.

Cruising at 80, he figured that by now the chicken was eating his dust but a glance in the side-view mirror revealed that the chicken was still right alongside.

Now the city slicker in the fast Italian sports car was completely flustered. He pushed the pedal to the metal and the 300 horsepower, fuel-injected engine revved up to its top speed, 160 miles per hour!

"Well, it took everything I had but at least I finally lost that darn chicken!" the driver thought to himself just before seeing the chicken streak past him and disappear over the next hill.

The driver was so shook up that he had to stop on the side of the road by a farmhouse and pull himself together.

The farmer ambled out to see what was the matter and the city slicker was near tears.

"My fancy, imported $100,000 sports car was just beaten in a race with a three-legged chicken!" he sobbed.

"Hmmm," the farmer scratched his chin. "Must be one of mine."

"O-O-One of yours?" the city feller sputtered.

"E-yah," drawled the taciturn downeaster. "Everybody in the family likes drumsticks so we raise three-legged chickens."

"That's amazing!" replied the driver. "Tell me, how do they taste?"

And the farmer said, "Can't rightly say. 'Tain't never caught one yet."

* * * *

Down in Florida, one of the biggest plagues afflicting residents of the Sunshine State are hordes of visiting relatives.

One man on the Gulf Coast has reportedly found a way to solve the problem once and for all. He borrows money from his wealthy relatives and lends it to his poor relatives and now, none of them come around!

Out on the golf course, a businessman was playing golf with a priest when a sudden storm blew up. The desperate pair found shelter in an old toolshed with a leaky roof and as the lightning struck all around them, they saw a roaring tornado bearing down on the shed.

"Father," said the businessman, "I don't want to die. Can't you do something about this?"

"Sorry," the priest replied, "I'm in sales, not management."

* * * *

Pot Shots

At a testimonial honoring a millionaire for his contributions to the Atlantic City community, the guest of honor wound up his speech by saying, "There was a time when I had sunk so low, I had to borrow a dime from a kind soul to use the men's room. When I went in, however, I discovered that someone had left the stall door ajar and so afterwards, I had the dime to drop in a progressive slot machine and win the jackpot. That win provided me with the capital to build my empire. I always say that if I ever encounter that kind person again, I'll share half my vast fortune with him."

From the back of the auditorium came a voice. "It's me! It's me! I'm the man who lent you that dime!"

"Sorry, Pal," said the quick-thinking millionaire. "The guy I'm looking for is the one who left the stall open!"

* * * *

Overheard at a train station:

Passenger: Pardon me. How long will the train be? Man at Ticket Window: Oh, about 12 cars and a caboose.

After a visit to New York City, the Pope was being taken back to Kennedy Airport in a chauffeur-driven limousine.

Halfway there the Pope leaned forward and tapped his driver on the shoulder. "Excuse me," said the Pontiff, "but I have never driven a car in my life. This is such a beautiful automobile, I wonder if I might drive it for awhile?"

"Well, I don't know, Your Holiness," replied the chauffeur hesitantly. "These streets are pretty rough and the traffic's terrible this time of day."

"Please allow me to drive just a couple of miles and I will be eternally grateful," pressed the Pope.

"Well, okay I guess," said the driver and he pulled over so that the Pope and he could change places.

A few minutes later, the Pope's little joyride came to an end when he was pulled over by a traffic cop.

The officer approached the vehicle but as soon as he saw the Pope roll down the window, he turned and went back to his car to contact headquarters on the radio.

"Hello, Sarge, this is Riley. I just pulled over a limo with somebody awfully important in it and I need instructions as to how to proceed."

"That important, eh?" said the Sarge. "Who is it, the President?"

"Naw. More important than that!"

"Don't tell me it's Frank Sinatra?"

"Nope. Even more important than that."

"I can't believe it! You better tell me exactly who this is you've stopped."

"That's just it, Sarge. I don't know who he is but he's got to be mighty important. He's got the Pope as his chauffeur!"

Thoughts from the Throne

"The trouble with unemployment is that the minute you wake up in the morning you're on the job."

—Slappy White

An import-export firm ran a help-wanted ad in the paper for a very exacting job and got only one applicant—a dog. Now the personnel manager certainly didn't want to hire a dog but he knew that the vague wording of the Equal Employment Opportunity Act might, in the hands of a shrewd lawyer, be made to apply to canines and so he didn't dare discriminate simply on the basis of species.

"Well, Mr. Rover," began the interviewer, "you see this job requires a minimum typing speed of 150 words per minute."

The dog went to the nearest typewriter and in the next 60 seconds banged out 175 words.

"Impressive," said the personnel manager. "But you also have to do extensive computer programming."

The dog immediately whipped out three manuals and a textbook that he'd written on the subject.

"Hmm, well, I must say that you're proficient enough in that department but . . ." the executive moved to the edge of his seat to deliver what he was sure would be the coup-de-grace. "We're an import-export firm and we have a very strict foreign language requirement."

The dog looked him right in the eye, smiled and said, "Meow."

* * * *

During a spate of civil unrest in Northern Flugelstein, the government secretly hired a couple of American mercenaries as bounty hunters and paid them 1000 Flugelmarks per captured terrorist member.

By the end of the month, the Americans, George and Charlie, had managed to nail about a half-dozen minor operatives of the Flugel Freedom Force. They were after bigger game, though, so they went to a deserted area about 20 miles outside of Flugeltown that was rumored to be an FFF stronghold.

Camping out in the forest the first night, one of the bounty hunters awoke in the morning to see that they were surrounded by 200 members of the FFF with automatic weapons, grenades and bazookas trained on them.

"Wake up, George!" cried Charlie excitedly. "We're rich!"

* * * *

Two Chicago tourists, heading to Florida for summer vacation had been tooling down hot, dry and dusty roads for hours when they happened to spot a tranquil little spring-fed pond. Sitting on the bank, a little barefoot boy was fishing.

"Yo Kid!" called one of the tourists. "Are there any snakes in this pond?"

"No, Sir," said the apple-cheeked lad.

"Great!" said the other tourist and the two dusty and overheated men stripped down to their BVDs and dove in the water.

After frollicking for a few minutes, one of the men surfaced near the boy and said, "Say, Son, I was just wondering. How do you know for sure that there aren't any snakes in this water?"

"Easy," the lad smiled. "The 'gators ate 'em all."

Thoughts from the Throne

"Cleaning your house while your kids are still growing is like shoveling the walk before it stops snowing."
—*Phyllis Diller*

Down in the canyons of Wall Street, a fabulously wealthy stockbroker passed a bedraggled beggar dressed in rags.

"Please, Sir, may I trouble you for a dollar so that I might get a bite to eat?" pleaded the bum.

"You poor fellow," said the stockbroker. "Listen. Come with me and I'll buy you a drink."

"Actually, Sir, I don't drink, but I would like a bit to eat."

"Here, my good man. Take one of my special stock of Cuban cigars," urged the broker.

"Sorry, Sir," said the bum. "I don't smoke."

"Well, listen then. Come with me down to Atlantic City. I'll stake you in the casino and you might win enough to get your life back on track."

"I can't do that, Sir. I don't gamble, but I would still like a bit to eat."

"You want to eat?" asked the stockbroker. "Very well, come home with me and have dinner with us."

"That's very kind of you, Sir. Thank you."

"Not at all," replied the broker. "I just want my wife to see what happens to a man who doesn't drink, smoke or gamble!"

MISCELLANEOUS MIRTH

Calling all cars! Calling all cars! Jailbreak at County Prison. Escapee described as a 4 foot 2 inch fortune teller. Be on the lookout for a small medium at large!

* * * *

During the winter you should always wash your clothes in Tide. Why? Because it's too darn cold out-tide, that's why!!

* * * *

A guy went to the dentist for the first time in 20 years.
"My gosh!" said the dentist peering down into the man's mouth.
"What a deep cavity! What a deep cavity!"
"You don't have to say it twice," growled the annoyed patient.
And the dentist replied, "I only said it once!"

* * * *

The sign on the way into the IRS office says "Watch Your Step."
On the way out it says "Watch Your Mouth."

* * * *

Then there's the fellow who discovered the best way to ward off Hare Krishnas at the airport. He had a sticker made for all his luggage which said, "I gave in a previous lifetime."

* * * *

One day a cannibal had a ferocious case of heartburn. He went to the witch doctor who told him that he must have eaten someone who disagreed with him.

* * * *

Two dogs were walking down the street. The Basset Hound says to the Pekinese, "Boy, have I got troubles. My master is cruel; my mate is sneaking around with a Saint Bernard; I'm suffering from feelings of inadequacy and my nerves are at the breaking point." "Why don't you go see a psychiatrist?" suggested the Pekinese. "Can't," answered the sad-sack Bassett Hound. "I'm not allowed on the couch."

* * * *

There was a terrible crash as the yuppie's car skidded off the road at a high speed and smashed into a huge oak tree. The police were on the scene minutes later and a cop was kneeling down beside the driver who had been thrown clear of the wreckage.

"Hold on, Buddy, the ambulance is coming," said the cop trying to comfort the victim.

"Oh, my poor Beamer, oh, my poor Beamer," moaned the yuppie.

"Listen, Mister," replied the cop. "I wouldn't worry about your car just now. In case you haven't noticed, your right arm has been ripped off and is laying over in those bushes!"

"It is?" responded the yuppie in horror. "Oh, my poor Rolex, oh, my poor Rolex."

* * * *

Two guys were in a psychiatrist's waiting room. One turned to the other and said, "What's your problem?"

"I'm a schizophrenic," came the reply.

"Well," said the first man, obviously pleased. "That makes four of us!"

* * * *

And then there was the car salesman who stood behind every car he sold. Somebody had to help push.

Thoughts from the Throne

"My parents put a live teddy bear in my crib."
—*Woody Allen*

A bit of bird-brained humor . . .

A bunch of ostriches decided to throw a surprise party honoring one of their own down by the lake. At the appointed hour, the ostrich of honor, thinking that they were attending a meeting, showed up at the fringe of the lakeshore.

"Here he comes!" the lookout ostrich whispered. "Quick everybody. Get your heads in the sand!"

* * * *

Manny Fishbein was a grizzled New York agent who had seen it all in his 50 years in show-biz. He was the top agent in town and getting on his client list meant a sure ticket to the big time so every two-bit act with big eyes for the bright lights of fame and fortune beat a path to Manny's door.

One Friday afternoon just before quitting time, a young man showed up at Manny's deceptively shabby office and announced, "I have the act of the century!" and with that, he began flapping his arms faster and faster, until he took off. He zoomed around the room once or twice, swooped out the open window and did double loops and barrel rolls over Broadway. Finally, as a finale, he went into a power dive, scattered the people on the sidewalk, soared back up to the 10th floor office and landed with a flourish in the chair in front of Manny's desk.

The old agent looked up at the lad and shrugged, "So that's all you do—bird imitations?"

* * * *

In a small New England town, a medicine show pitchman was hauled in for selling phony youth pills.

"You're in a lot of trouble, Son," said the straight arrow police detective in his best Joe Friday monotone. "Frankly, I'm amazed that people still fall for these scams in this day and age but just because your customers are gullible doesn't make fraud any less a crime."

Just then the cop's partner came in and said, "You were right, Joe. He's got priors on this youth pill scam. Seems he was arrested on the same charge in 1743, 1868 and 1973!"

* * * *

The World's CLEANEST Traveling Salesman Joke . . .

Harry went to see his old buddy in Chicago who still ran the little corner grocery store that his father started a half century ago.

Stepping into the store, Harry shook hands with his friend and they brought each other up to date. But Harry seemed distracted.

The shelves of the store were all filled with soap. And as his friend showed Harry around the place, he couldn't help but notice that the stockroom was filled with soap; the basement was filled with soap; the living quarters over the store were filled with soap and out back, there was a 50 foot storage trailer filled with soap.

"Gee, pal," said Harry shaking his head. "You sure do sell a lot of soap here!"

"Nah, not really," replied his friend. "But the guy who sold it to me—brother, could he sell soap!"

Thoughts from the Throne

"Anyone who says he can see through women is missing a lot."

—Groucho Marx

A Quick Trip to the Laughroom . . .

Although the bathroom is no place for "stand up" humor, here are a few chuckles to pass the time . . .

Semi-retired, Evel Knievel now runs a Pied Piper service for lawyers. He goes from town to town and drives an ambulance off a cliff!!!

* * * *

An old Indian sending smoke signals in the Southwestern Desert back in the 50's felt an earth-shaking blast and looked up to see the enormous mushroom cloud of a nuclear test rising high into the stratosphere. He gazed at the cloud, shook his head and sent up the message: "You don't have to yell!"

* * * *

Almost 30 years later, that same noble Native American was communing with nature while trekking through the Cascades. As it happens, he was about ten miles away from Mount St. Helens at the moment that it blew its lid. The old brave glanced over his shoulder to see a tremendous plume of smoke and ash rising into the sky. "Gee," he thought. "I wish I'd have said that."

* * * *

Then there was the guy who invented a glow-in-the-dark sundial so folks could see to use it at night.

You know of course that in Tibet, the Lama, as in Dali Lama, is spelled with one "1." The South American animal has a double "1" in its name but do you know what a three "1" lama is?
One heck of a big fire!

* * * *

A guy who was tired of being called "monkey-puss" inherited $10,000 and decided that he'd invest it in improving his appearance. He went to a plastic surgeon, plunked down the cash and said, "Give me whatever you think I need most." A few hours later, he woke up in the recovery room and ran to the mirror. His face was just as bad as ever. He could tell that he didn't even have a tummy tuck or a hair transplant and so he barged back into the surgeon's office and demanded to know what he got for the money.
"Well, my good fellow, you asked me to give you whatever you needed most and I did," replied the doctor.
"Yeah?" came the belligerent reply. "Well, then, where is it?"
"Look behind you," said the surgeon. "You'll see that I added a tail!"

* * * *

Two seagulls were flying over the stables at Hialeah Race Track when one looked down and said, "I'm going to put everything I have on number 7!"

* * * *

A little kid was watching a wedding on TV and asked, "Daddy, how much does it cost to get married?"
His father looked up from his newspaper and snorted, "I can't answer that, Son. I'm STILL paying for it!"

* * * *

Q: What do fans of Morris the Cat call the '70's?
A: The Meow Decade.

* * * *

The wealthy lightbulb manufacturer donated his products, free of charge, for use on all the theater marquees in New York. Seems he always wanted to see his lights up in names . . .

Pot Shots

Out in the tropical South Pacific many years ago, a ship carrying luxury toilets ran aground on a beautiful isle populated by primitive natives. When the chief discovered the ship's cargo, he had several dozen of the bejeweled johns taken to his hut and locked in his specially-built attic. One night, while the chief lay sleeping, the ceiling gave way and he was crushed under the tumbling toilies. All of which goes to prove the old adage: "People who live in grass houses shouldn't stow thrones."

* * * *

Then there was the tattoo artist who was fired for having designs on her clients.

* * * *

"What does your husband do?"
"Odd jobs."
"Odd jobs, really?"
"Yep, if he's got a job, it's odd!"

Back in the early days of aviation, a pilot radioed a MAYDAY signal.

"Control tower, this is XYZ 40 en route to Chicago. There's a large hole in the bottom of my gas tank and I fear that my fuel loss will cause me to crash before I can reach an airport."

"Then fly upside down," came the cool reply from the tower.

The pilot complied and reached the airport safely. The moral is: "Loop before you leak!"

Thoughts from the Throne

"Be careful about reading health books—you might die from a misprint."

—*Mark Twain*

* * * *

One day the boss was approached by a longtime employee who began working for the firm where his grandfather began it decades before.

"Sir, I wonder if I might have a word with you?" the old man wheezed. "Coming up the beginning of next month is my 50th anniversary with the company and I was just wondering if I could have the day off to celebrate with some old co-workers up at the retirement home."

"Well, all right," growled the boss. "But don't go expecting this every 50 years!"

* * * *

Patient: Doc, everybody takes advantage of me!
Psychiatrist: That's quite normal.
Patient: Really? That's great! How much do I owe you?
Psychiatrist: How much have you got?

Although the head of the giant bio-technology corporation loved his work dearly, he regretted not having more time to spend with his family so he went to his chief research scientist and asked him to come up with a solution.

"That's quite simple, Sir. All you need is a clone of yourself to handle the business details and you'll have plenty of time at home."

The executive thought that was great and so the scientist took some cells from the inside of his mouth and began the cloning process.

Six months later, the clone was ready and the CEO was anxious to meet his double, but the scientist cautioned him, "Sir, I must tell you that the cloning and accelerated growth procedures that we use aren't completely perfected yet. Your clone is exact in every detail except that it has an unfortunate tendency towards foul language."

Figuring that the head of a huge corporation needed a pretty salty vocabulary anyway, the executive didn't blink an eye and left for home to enjoy family life as his clone took over.

It wasn't long before trouble broke out. Longtime employees were quitting and suing for sexual harrassment. The double's foul mouth had offended and lost many major clients and his vulgar tongue was proving to be a disaster to the business.

Knowing that he had to do something and fast, the CEO called his double and asked for a meeting at the restaurant atop company headquarters.

The two met and over lunch their argument became more and more heated. The swear words literally poured out of the genetically engineered garbage mouth. He must have run through about every filthy word in the book when the original CEO, completely fed up, hauled off and belted him. The force knocked the double through a plate glass window and he plummeted 30 stories to the sidewalk below.

Within minutes the police showed up and took the CEO into custody and the executive demanded to know the charge.

"That should be obvious, Sir," the cop said. "You're being arrested for making an obscene clone fall."

❋　❋　❋　❋

At the start of World War II, supplies were scarce so when one of the first inductees showed up at boot camp he was given a broomstick.

"Just pretend that it's your rifle, Recruit," barked the drill sergeant. "When you see the enemy coming just point it and shout 'Bangity-bangity bang'!"

The next week, the recruit was handed a banana and the sergeant said, "Just pretend that it's a bayonet. Attach it to the end of your broomstick and if you find yourself in hand-to-hand combat just thrust it forward and say, 'Stabbity-stabbity-stab'."

Well, the recruit was more than a little nervous when he was shipped out to fight and the rifles and the bayonets still hadn't arrived but his sergeant reassured him by telling him to just remember the instructions for the broomstick and banana.

The private soon found himself in battle and sure enough, when he saw the Nazis coming over the hill he pointed his broomstick and shouted 'Bangity-bangity-bang' and the enemy fell dead by the dozens. The charge kept up however, and the soldier soon was battling in close quarters so he tied the banana to the broomstick and walked around jabbing at the air and shouting 'Stabbity-stabbity-stab.' As he did the Nazis bit the dust—all but one. He just kept on coming. 'Bangity-bangity-bang' didn't slow him one bit and neither did 'Stabbity-stabbity-stab.' The private was trying to decide whether to retreat or surrender when the enemy soldier knocked him down and walked over his back. As he was getting stomped into the mud the G.I. heard the German growling in a low voice, "Tankity-tankity-tank."

Thoughts from the Throne

"The temperature in any room is room temperature."
—Steven Wright

A novice skydiver bailed out of a plane 5000 feet up in the big Montana sky. He was enjoying the experience immensely until he pulled the rip cord and his parachute failed to open. Panicking, he then pulled the cord on his reserve chute and that failed to open as well.

In utter despair, he started making peace with his Maker but he happened to open his eyes long enough to notice that there was someone just alongside him—just hanging there seemingly motionless.

"Oh, praise Heaven!" the skydiver cried. "You're my guardian angel, sent here to tell me how to get my parachute open!"

"I don't know nuthin' 'bout no parachutes, Buddy," answered the figure. "But maybe you could clue me in on the right way to light a gas stove."

* * * *

Ralph, the burly but brainless construction worker, was riveting the superstructure of a new high-rise when his head started to itch. He removed his hardhat to scratch but just at that moment a girder came swinging by on a cable and tore off his ear. Leaning over the edge, he called to his coworkers below, "Hey, have any of you guys seen my ear?"

"Yeah, it's over here near the cement mixer," came a reply from below.

"Naw, that's not it," called Ralph. "Mine had a pencil behind it!"

* * * *

Two guys were walking down the Boardwalk in Atlantic City late one night counting up their casino winnings when a man jumped out of the shadows with a gun and demanded all their money. As they were cleaning out their wallets, one guy turned to the other and said, "Oh, by the way, here's that $20 I owe you."

* * * *

A guy dashes into a psychiatrist's office, throws himself to couch and says, "Doc, ya gotta help me. I think I'm a biscuit. What do you think?" The shrink strokes his chin thoughtfully and asks, "Are you square?"

"Yes."

"Do you have lots of little holes?"

"Yes! Yes!"

"And are you covered all over with a light sprinkling of salt?"

"Yes! Yes! Yes!"

"Then you're not a biscuit—you're crackers!"

* * * *

One day, two female William Morris agents were out jogging in the woods near their homes when they passed a small pond and heard a voice.

"Help me, please!"

They looked around but saw no one. They were just about to continue on when they heard, "Help me, please!" again.

This time one of the women noticed that the plea was coming from a frog sitting on a lily pad. This was one ugly frog—ugly as a toad, actually. But he had a beautiful voice and said, "Ladies, I beg of you to help me. I was once the greatest street performer in Paris, a mime who was famous all over the Continent, but a wicked witch cast a spell on me and changed me into the lowly creature you see before you. All I need to break the spell is a kiss from a beautiful woman and I'll turn back into what I once was."

One of the women, apparently feeling a great surge of pity, bent down, scooped up the tiny amphibian in her hand, brought him near her lips and then stuck him in her sweatsuit pocket.

"Why didn't you kiss him and break the spell?" her shocked companion asked.

"Because," she answered, "I can make a heckuva lot more on a talking frog than from some stupid street mime!"

* * * *

Thoughts from the Throne

*"Nobody goes to that restaurant.
It's too crowded."*
—*Yogi Berra*

Conversation by the water cooler: "By the way, Joe, how long have you been working here?" "Ever since they threatened to fire me!"

※ ※ ※ ※

After a long hard day on the links, the tired golfer returned home to a tirade from his nagging wife.
"Oh, be quiet, Janice, or you'll drive me out of my mind!" he finally snapped.
"In your case, my dear," she sneered sweetly, "that wouldn't be a drive. That would be a putt!"

※ ※ ※ ※

And then there was the one about the Calcutta dentist who used to be a maharishi. He doesn't use novacaine because he can transcend dental medication . . .

※ ※ ※ ※

And then there was the guy who had an extremely short career in the exciting field of convenience store robberies. His first time out, he had his wife's panty hose over his face. The trouble was, his wife was still wearing them!

Stopping to ask directions at a farmhouse, a traveling salesman noticed a pig with a wooden leg snoozing on the front porch.

"If you don't mind me asking," he said to the farmer, "how come that pig has a wooden leg?"

"Three years ago," answered the farmer matter-of-factly, "there was a flood and that pig swam across a raging torrent, grabbed me by the collar and pulled me to shore."

"That's amazing! But what about the wooden leg?"

"Two years ago," said the farmer, "the house caught on fire and that pig crashed through the front window, found me unconscious on the floor and carried me to safety on his back."

"Wow! That's really something, but what about the leg?" persisted the salesman.

"Just last year," the farmer replied, "a gang of escaped convicts tried to take me hostage but that pig snuck up from behind with my shotgun and got the drop on them. His picture was in all the papers."

"Yes, yes, yes!" sputtered the frustrated stranger. "BUT WHAT ABOUT THAT WOODEN LEG?"

"Well, you see," drawled the farmer. "A pig like that you don't eat all at once."

Thoughts from the Throne

"Have you noticed? Anybody driving slower than you is an idiot, and anyone going faster than you is a moron."

—George Carlin

At his 50th wedding anniversary party, Grandpa Rosenthal was asked the secret of his long marriage. He stood up before his assembled crowd of friends and relatives and shared his marital philosophy.

"Martha and I have made it a practice throughout our long marriage to go out for two romantic, candlelit dinners a week. Unfailingly, twice a week, we go out, enjoy the delicious food and soft susic. We soak up the ambiance of a fine restaurant and sip a vintage wine. She goes Thursdays and I go Fridays."

Nuts to Soup . . .

One of the staples of the comedy menu over the years has been the old 'Waiter, there's a fly in my soup . . .' gag, and some versions are truly enough to gag you . . .

"Waiter, there's a fly in my soup!"
"Please be quiet, Sir, everyone will want one!"

* * * *

"Waiter, there's a fly in my soup!"
"Sorry, Sir, that's our Nouvelle Cuisine Thanksgiving turkey."

* * * *

"Waiter, there's a fly swimming in my soup!"
"How fortunate, Sir. There's usually only enough soup for them to wade."

* * * *

"Waiter, there's a fly in my soup!"
"Don't worry, the tarantula will come up under him any moment now."

* * * *

"Waiter, there's a fly in my soup!"
"I'm sorry, Sir, that's chicken noodle. You should have gotten the cockroach with that!"

* * * *

"Waiter, what's this fly doing in my soup?"
"Looks like the backstroke."

* * * *

"Waiter, there's a fly at the bottom of my soup!"
"I like to save them for last myself, Sir!"

* * * *

Frog: "Hey Waiter! There's no fly in my soup!"

* * * *

"Waiter, there's a fly in my soup!"
"You're lucky that it's not HALF a fly!"

* * * *

"Waiter, there's a fly in my soup!"
"Oh, heavens no, Sir. He's not in your soup. He's been stuck to that bowl for weeks!"

* * * *

"Waiter, there's a fly in my soup!"
"So vhat do you vant? A fork, maybe?"

"Waiter, what's this fly doing in my alphabet soup?"
"Seems like he's sending an S.O.S."

* * * *

"Waiter, there's a fly in my soup!"
"Don't worry, Sir. He's used to the heat."

* * * *

"Waiter, there's a fly in my soup!"
"Yes, sir! That's our famous slow-cooking soup. He's been there ever since he was just a little maggot!"

* * * *

And to a server who just spilled a bowl of steaming broth in an annoyed customer's lap, "Waiter, there's a soup in my fly!"

After a minor fender bender on a lonely highway, the two vehicles pulled to the side of the road and the drivers went through the familiar ritual of exchanging licenses, insurance cards and the like.

"Say," said one, "you look all shook up. I've got a bottle of scotch in my car. Have some to soothe your nerves."

"Thanks," replied the other driver taking a mighty swig. "Won't you be having any?"

"Not until after the cops get here."

* * * *

Patient: Doc, you gotta help me. My wife thinks she's an elevator.
Psychiatrist: Bring her in to see me.
Patient: I can't. She doesn't stop at this floor!

Thoughts from the Throne

"Cannibal—a guy who goes into a restaurant and orders the waiter."

—Jack Benny

Crazy Mel of Crazy Mel's Unpainted Furniture fame went to the bank for a loan but he was mortgaged to the hilt and had no collateral.

"What assurance does the bank have that you'll pay this loan back?" asked the dour loan officer.

"Won't a gentleman's word of honor do?" asked Crazy Mel.

"It might," answered the banker. "Now, where are you going to find one?"

* * * *

The dutiful daughter showed up at the house with a man who was naked except for a carved wooden mask, a spear, some feathers and a loincloth. Looking like an extra from an old jungle movie, the man chanted, danced and sprinkled powdered monkey brains all over the furniture.

"Well, here he is, Mother," she beamed. "The man of our dreams. I met him this morning and just so he shouldn't get away, I married him this afternoon!"

Her mother was totally horrified. "Why? Why him?" she cried.

"But, Mother," answered her confused daughter. "He's just the type of man you always said that you wanted me to marry."

Her mother shook her head and groaned, "I said RICH doctor, darn it, RICH doctor!"

* * * *

One night at dinner, a boy who had never spoken a word in his 17 years pushed his plate away and said, "The succotash is too salty!"

His parents were thunderstruck.

"You can talk!" gushed his mother. "Why haven't you ever said anything before?"

"Up to now," the teenager replied, "everything's been ok."

* * * *

Sir Edmund Smith-Smythe, the famed mountain climber, was challenging one of Africa's highest peaks, a volcano which recently had become active again.

Scaling the sheer cliff above the roiling crater, he lost his footing. His safety rope snapped and he plunged 200 feet before grabbing a tiny tree—a twig really—sprouting in a space between the rocks. Dangling there helplessly, staring straight down into the hellish magma, he lost his famed British reserve. Sir Edmund cried out, "Oh God! If there's anyone up in heaven, help me!"

In a voice deeper than the volcano's, came the answer. "Sir Edmund, the most important thing is for you to have faith. You must believe what I say. Now, let go of the branch."

Sir Edmund glanced down into the bubbling cauldron of magma thousands of feet below, then looked back up to the sky and yelled, "I say, is anyone else up there?"

* * * *

Thoughts from the Throne

"What a good thing Adam had — when he said a good thing, he knew nobody had said it before."

—*Mark Twain*

Ralph went to an estate auction and spotted a beautiful parrot about to come up on the block.

"What a gorgeous bird!" he thought. "That's the perfect anniversary gift for my wife—and I'll probably get it cheap. After all, who wants a used bird?"

The bidding began and Ralph signaled $5.

Another bidder raised it to $10.

Ralph countered with $15.

The other bidder upped it to $25.

As the bidding accelerated, Ralph lost sight of the fact that he was originally looking for a bargain. Instead, the bidding war became a matter of pride and he was carried away with the moment.

Soon the price was up to $1800 and Ralph bid $1850.

Then there was silence. The auctioneer gaveled the sale to a conclusion. Ralph wrote a check and took the overpriced bird home.

When he got there, he sat in the living room for an hour saying things like 'Polly want a cracker? Pretty bird. Hello, hello?'

The bird was silent. Not a peep.

Finally in frustration, Ralph jumped to his feet and yelled at the bird. "Look at you. I shell out $1850 for you and you can't even talk!"

"Can't even talk?" replied the parrot. "Who do you think was bidding against you?"

* * * *

He: I accidentally swallowed my watch.
She: Does it hurt?
He: Only when I try to wind it.

* * * *

Husband: Your Honor, I want a divorce. My wife threw my new suit out our third story window.
Judge: Well, that doesn't seem so bad.
Husband: I was wearing it at the time!

* * * *

Fred had an old Datsun and he loved the little car even though it was getting worn out and parts were scarce. Finally, one day his mechanic told him that the engine needed a new cog and that the cog was very hard to get.

After calling auto parts houses for weeks, Fred finally came to the conclusion that he'd have to fly over to the main parts depot in Japan and get the cog himself.

Arriving at the warehouse outside of Tokyo, he decided to buy several dozen of the cogs just so he'd have a lifetime supply.

That afternoon, he was back on the plane, heading for home and just as the plane flew over the west coast, it developed engine trouble and the captain announced that, in order to lighten the plane, all the baggage had to be jettisoned including Fred's cogs.

Down below, in a sleepy little town where nothing much ever happened, an old couple were sitting on the front porch in rocking chairs. Suddenly, the old geezer squinted at the falling debris all around the house and said to his wife, "Look, Lizzie, it's raining Datsun cogs!"

Thoughts from the Throne

"The formula for water is H_2O. Is the formula for an ice cube H_2O squared?"

—Lily Tomlin

A man who just turned 80 is talking to his son. "My boy, you know I'm pretty lucky. I've got my health. Heart's good; kidneys are workin' fine; lungs are clear and my mind, knock wood . . . who's there?"

During spring training in Florida, a horse shows up at tryouts and says to the manager, "Hey, Pal, give me a shot and I guarantee you the pennant this year."

Well, the manager is taken aback by both the talking horse and his extravagant claim but he tells the horse to step up to the plate and motions the pitcher to burn one in.

Holding the bat in his mouth, the horse connects with the ball and sends it out of the stadium.

"Amazing!" says the manager. "Let's try him on pitching."

The horse strides out to the mound and pitches the ball with a quick twist of his head and manages to strike out 10 batters in a row.

"Sensational!" yells the manager. "Now we'll check your fielding."

Sure enough, the horse just couldn't miss and made impossible catch after impossible catch. The manager signed him up on the spot.

The next day, the team has an exhibition game and the manager brings out the horse as his secret weapon pinch-hitter. The bases are loaded and the horse steps up to the plate, takes a swing and blasts one right over the wall. Then he just stands there.

The manager comes running out of the dugout screaming at the horse, "Run! Run! You stupid plug!"

The horse looks at him indignantly and says, "Hey, Buddy, if I could run, I'd be at Hialeah!"

❋　❋　❋　❋

Thoughts from the Throne

"A vegetarian is a person who won't eat anything that can have children."

—David Brenner

❋　❋　❋　❋

JOKE-PARDY

Steve Allen did the bit as "The Question Man." Johnny Carson put it in a turban and gave us "Carnac The Magnificent" for 30 years. Merv Griffin even used the gimmick to create the classic game show "Jeopardy." And so with a respectful nod to the pioneers of this premise, "The Bathroom Joke Book" proudly presents Joke-pardy. We give you the answer and you try to guess the question . . .

1. Answer: Gunga Din
   And the Question?

2. Answer: Pen Pals
   And the Question?

3. Answer: Yabba Dabba Doo
   And the Question?

4. Answer: A Wagoneer, the Marianas Trench and Saddam Hussein
   And the Question?

5. Answer: Camelot
   And the Question?

6. Answer: Rub a Dub Dub
   And the Question?

7. Answer: Chicken Teriyaki
   And the Question?

8. Answer: Computer Virus
   And the Question?

9. Answer: Pin Money
   And the Question?

10. Answer: Pandemonium
    And the Question?

Questions to Joke-pardy

1. *What noise will result if you bang your gungas together?*

2. *What did Lawrence Welk get on his face as a teenager?*

3. *What often forms on your Yabba Dabba early in the morning?*

4. *Name a Jeep, a deep and a creep.*

5. *Where does the Emir of Kuwait park his camel?*

6. *How might you shine up a dub dub?*

7. *Name the only kamikaze pilot to survive the war.*

8. *What's the main thing to watch out for while computer dating?*

9. *What's the best way to pay your acupuncturist?*

10. *What do they call retirement hi-rises for pandas in Florida?*

Pot Shots

One night at a popular local pub, the bartender was taken aback when he saw a group of small swine come in and start ordering beers. About every other round or so, he noticed all but one of the pigs trekking back to the bathrooms. This went on all through the evening up until the last call at which point the barkeep couldn't contain his curiousity any longer.

"Tell me," he asked the pig who hadn't moved off the barstool all night. "I couldn't help but notice that while all your friends made several trips to the rest rooms, you downed beers all evening and never used the facilities. What's your secret?

"No secret, my good man," replied the semi-soused sow. "I'm just the little piggy that goes wee-wee-wee all the way home."

At the stylish boutique on Rodeo Drive in the swankiest shopping area in the country, the sales clerk brought out a sequined and jeweled gown for a customer.

"It's $5,000, Ma'am, and we guarantee a fit."

The woman took out her charge card and said, "I guarantee a fit too—when my husband gets the bill!"

* * * *

"Howdy, Pardner," said the grizzled old prospector to the 'citified' stranger sitting in the Silver Dollar Saloon. "What brings you to these parts?"

"Well, to tell you the truth, Fella, my mother decided that her sons were getting soft living back east so she bought us a big spread outside of town for a cattle ranch."

"Yeah? What's the name of your ranch?"

"Well, that's an interesting story. I was partial to the name Circle B. My wife wanted to call it the Bar Q. Then my older brother wanted the Double MM but his wife liked the Cross T. My younger brother insisted we call it the Circle A Bar X but his wife had her heart set on the Lost Dutchman. We finally decided to compromise and to keep everyone happy, we named it the Circle B Bar Q Double MM Cross T Circle A Bar X Lost Dutchman Cattle Ranch Inc."

"Quite a name!" observed Ol' Whiskers. "Tell me, how many head of cattle you got out there?"

"We don't have any, actually. So far, none of them has survived the branding!"

* * * *

A panic-stricken golfer charged into the clubhouse, grabbed the pro by the arm and said, "You gotta help! I was on the 9th hole and I hit a terrible slice. The ball sailed right off the course and hit a guy riding a motorcycle. He lost control and swerved into the path of a truck. The truck tried to stop but jack-knifed, rolled over and broke apart. It was carrying thousands of bee hives and now the angry bees are attacking everyone in sight. It's awful! It's a disaster! What should I do?"

And the pro answered, "Well, the first thing is you've got to keep your arms straight and remember to get your right hand a bit more under the club . . ."

Down at the stationhouse, a rookie cop hauled a little guy up in front of the sergeant. The man had a desk strapped to his back, was carrying a water cooler under his right arm, a typewriter under his left arm and was wearing a fax machine for a hat.

"What's the charge, Murphy?" growled the crusty old desk sergeant.

"Impersonating an office, Sir."

Thoughts from the Throne

"The worst gift is a fruitcake. There is only one fruitcake in the entire world, and people keep sending it to each other."

—*Johnny Carson*

A teenage yam arrived at home with the exciting news for her parents.

"I'm getting married!" gushed the starry-eyed young yam.

"To whom?" asked Mother Yam.

"David Brinkley."

"David Brinkley? You can't marry him!"

"Why not?" demanded her daughter.

"Because you are a yam and he's just a commen-tator!"

✳ ✳ ✳ ✳

First Farmer: Zeb, why in the world did you let that fast-talking salesman sign you up for two electric milking machines?

Second Farmer: He told me the deal was too good to pass up.

First Farmer: But you've only got one cow.

Second Farmer: Not any more. I used it as a down payment on the milking machines!

Jeff and Jack were on their first big camping trip and they were strolling through the wilderness, taking in the beauty of Yellowstone, when suddenly they spotted a grizzly bear in a clearing about a hundred feet away.

"Stand absolutely still," instructed Jack. "He may not see us."

The grizzly sniffed the air, spun in their direction and began charging at a full gallop.

"Okay, it's time to run," said Jack in a surprisingly calm voice.

"Why aren't you more frightened?" puffed Jeff as he dashed through the woods trying to keep up with Jack. "The ranger said that these bears can run 40 miles an hour. We'll never outrun him."

"That's just it, Jeff," Jack called back over his shoulder. "I don't have to outrun him. I only have to outrun YOU!"

* * * *

A disgruntled customer stepped up to a grocery store courtesy counter and said, "I want to return the milk I bought here yesterday. It's outdated."

"How can you tell?" asked the clerk.

"Because the missing person on the carton is Amelia Earhart!"

* * * *

A man was cleaning out the attic of his grandfather's house when he found a shoe repair ticket dated 1912. As it happened, the repair shop was still in business and so the grandson, in order to have a bit of fun, made a trip downtown to claim the shoes.

Walking into the store, he presented the ticket to the clerk and waited for the reaction. The clerk didn't say a word, went in the back for a minute, came out and announced, "Yes, we have them, Sir. They'll be ready next Tuesday."

* * * *

A loving and devoted couple were looking forward to the big Halloween costume ball for months and even went so far as to rent matching gorilla costumes. When the time came to leave, however, Louise was stricken with one of her killer migraines but insisted that her husband go on ahead without her.

After an hour nap, Louise was feeling better and so she put on her costume and went to the party, excited about how surprised her husband would be.

Spotting the other gorilla, Louise walked up and motioned him to the terrace. The two gorillas danced together and then Louise gave a few fetching gorilla grunts, took his hand and led him out onto the deserted beach. Soon, with the moonlight working its magic, they were locked in a passionate embrace gorilla suits and all—and engaging in monkey business of the highest order.

After their tryst, the two gorillas walked hand in hand back to the party to mingle but Louise, exhausted from her workout, took the opportunity to slip away and returned home.

Later, when her husband came home from the party, he found her propped up in bed reading. Deciding to play it coy, Louise purred, "How was the party, Dear?"

"Okay, I guess," came his rather noncommittal reply.

"OKAY, YOU GUESS?" She was highly insulted. "What do you mean by that?"

"Well, I couldn't get into it without you, Honey, so I spent the evening playing poker in the back room." Then he brightened and added, "But wait till you hear what happened to the guy I loaned the costume to!"

* * * *

Thoughts from the Throne

"I don't like to watch golf on television. I can't stand whispering."

—David Brenner

Doc-Doc Jokes

Okay, now for some medical mirth. These jokes represent a smattering of doctor gags that have been popular over the years. Some date back, in one form or another, to the dim, dark past when doctors would bleed patients with leeches. Others range all the way up to modern times when the bleeding is done with fees . . .

* * * *

Patient: Hey Doc, ya gotta help me. I think I'm losing my memory!
Doctor: I see. How long have you had this problem?"
Patient: What problem?

* * * *

First Man: You should go see my doctor. He's very reasonable.
Second Man: How so?
First Man: Well, if you can't afford the operation, he touches up the X-rays.

* * * *

Doctor: My diagnosis is that there's nothing wrong with you. You're just plain stupid.
Patient: If you don't mind, I'd like a second opinion.
Doctor: All right, you're ugly, too.

* * * *

Man: Hey, Doc, it hurts when I do this.
Doc: Well, then, don't do that!

* * * *

Patient: I just don't know what's worse—having my teeth drilled or having a baby!
Dentist: Well, make up your mind, Lady. I've got to know how to adjust the chair!

* * * *

Patient: I don't know what's wrong, Doc. My teeth chattered all night.
Doctor: What'd you do?
Patient: Well, I finally had to get up and take them out of the glass!

* * * *

An old man goes to the doctor and after the examination the medico says, "Mr. Jones, you're healthy as a horse. You'll live to be 90."
To which the patient replies, "I AM 90!"
And the doctor says, "See, what'd I tell you?"

* * * *

Doctor: Hmmm, your cough sounds a lot better.
Patient: It should. I practiced all night!

* * * *

Patient: (On phone) Hey, Doc, you know that stuff you gave me to spread on my scalp to make my hair grow heavy?
Doctor: The baldness treatment? Yeah, what about it?
Patient: Well, it worked. I've only got one hair but it weighs 20 pounds!

Doctor: What are you worried about? I had the same condition myself once and I recovered fully.

Worried Patient: Yeah, but you didn't have the same doctor!

* * * *

Doctor: Now remember, take this medicine only with meals. That'll be $50.

Destitute Patient: But Doc, I haven't eaten for a week!

Doctor: Fine, then the pills will last a lot longer.

* * * *

Patient: Hey Doc, would you give me something for my head?

Doctor: No, but there's a dental college around the corner that might be interested.

* * * *

A crestfallen man comes home from the doctor.

"What's wrong, Dear?" asks his wife.

"The doctor informed me that I've only got 8 hours to live. I'll tell you what—let's go out for the most expensive dinner in town and then we'll dance to dawn."

"Oh, that's great for you," the wife replies. "You don't have to get up in the morning."

* * * *

Patient: Hey Doc, when the bandages come off my hands will I be able to play the piano?

Doctor: Certainly.

Patient: Great. I always wanted to be able to play the piano!

Kramer goes to an optometrist and he's lead into a room where the doctor pulls down a small screen with letters.

"Read me the bottom line, Mr. Kramer."

"Sorry, Doc, I can't."

"Okay, how about the line above that?"

"Nope."

". . . the next one up?"

"Nope."

This goes on for half an hour with the optometrist pulling down progressively larger and larger eye charts with ever-bigger letters. Finally, the doctor says, "Well, I've never had to use it before, but see if you can read this."

With that, he pulled a lever, the wall collapsed and a giant 50 foot flaming orange "A" rose up out of the ground.

"Now surely you can read THAT!" snarled the frustrated optometrist.

"Sorry, Doc, but I can't."

"Then, man, you must be blind!"

"Oh no, Doc, my eyesight's fine. I just never learned how to read!"

✳ ✳ ✳ ✳

The doctor gave me 6 months to live. I told him that I'd never be able to pay his bill by then so he gave me another 6 months.

✳ ✳ ✳ ✳

I went to see my doctor last month and he said, "Don't worry. I'll have you walking in a week." Sure enough, the bill came in and I had to sell my car!

✳ ✳ ✳ ✳

Patient: Ya gotta help me, Doc! Nobody respects me.

Psychiatrist: How do you know?

Patient: I went into Burger King, ordered a Whopper and they made me have it THEIR way!

A woman brings her kid to the emergency room.

"Doctor, my son swallowed $4.75 in change."

"My, that's a lot of change. It's hard to believe the little devil could get it all down at once."

"Oh, he didn't, Doc. He's been swallowing it for a year."

"Why didn't you bring him in before?"

"I haven't needed the money until now!"

* * * *

That same tot was given an intestinal lubricant and admitted for observation. In the middle of the night his mother called to check on his condition.

"No change yet," reported the nurse.

* * * *

A guy walked into a doctor's office wearing a stovepipe hat the likes of which hadn't been seen since Lincoln's day. Taking it off, the doctor noticed a rose bush growing out of the fellow's head.

"My, my," said the medico. " I can certainly understand why you came to see me!"

"You ain't kidding, Doc," said the young patient. "These aphids are killing me!"

* * * *

Just had my yearly physical. I said, "Well, Doc, how do I stand?" And he said, "That's what puzzles me!"

Then there was the breakfast cereal executive who put out a new version of an old favorite, "Crackle Pop." Apparently he overstepped his authority—he was fired for making Snap decisions.

Thoughts from the Throne

*"Only one man in a thousand is a leader
of men — the other 999 follow women."*
—Groucho Marx

Two old friends met on the street.
"Hey, Frank, long time, no see."
"Yeah, what's new, Larry?"
"Well, I just got a new hearing aid—top of the line, state of the art."
"Really?"
"Yep," replied Larry proudly. "With its new microelectronic circuitry, this hearing aid also is a tiny radio allowing me to monitor AM, FM and shortwave broadcasts from all over the world. It's also a tiny calculator which instantly provides the solution to any spoken mathematical problem. And best of all, it's a tiny transceiver—a two-way radio that allows me to stay in constant touch with home or the office!"
"Wow! That's one great hearing aid," said Frank, highly impressed. "What kind is it?"
"Oh," replied Larry, "about quarter after two."

* * * *

Late at night, a doctor got an emergency phone call from one of his patients.
"Doc, listen, it's my wife. I think she's got appendicitis!"
"That's impossible!" replied the doctor somewhat annoyed at being disturbed for a false alarm.
"No, Doc, I tell you it looks like appendicitis," retorted the patient.
"Couldn't be," explained the doctor in a very condescending manner. "I took your wife's appendix out last year. Now, have you ever heard of anyone getting a second appendix?"
"Well, no, Doc," came the reply. "But have you ever heard of anyone getting a second wife?"

Mayor Tunney was famous for bloating the local public works payroll with his relatives and so it was that his eldest son got a summer job installing telephone poles way out in the country. After a few days though, the supervisor called him in and, mayor's son or not, demanded an explanation for his lack of productivity.

"Look, Kid," snorted the boss. "According to these worksheets, the other guy we've got putting in poles averages 12 a day. You go out with the same equipment for 8 hours and only manage to drive in 6. Now, I want you to go home tonight and think about what it is you're doing wrong."

The next morning the mayor's son showed up at the office and went in to see the boss.

"Listen, Boss, you had me up all night worrying about what I was doing wrong and I just couldn't figure it out. So I left early this morning and took a drive by the road where the other guy's putting in a dozen poles a day and suddenly it hit me how he does so many more."

"Oh, really?" said the boss, obviously pleased that he had gotten through to the lad. "What's his secret?"

"Easy. He only drives the poles in halfway!"

✳   ✳   ✳   ✳

Another one of the mayor's relatives landed a job on the local road crew and although the supervisor was used to the incompetence that nepotism usually breeds, he was completely baffled by this particular case.

"Tell me, Dennis," the foreman said calmly. "How it is that the first day you worked here, you painted five miles of line down the center of the road—almost a record. The next day, you only managed three miles and by quitting time today, you only laid down one measly mile of line?"

"Well, Boss," replied the mayor's favorite nephew, "you gotta remember that it's farther back to the paint can each time!"

Thoughts from the Throne

"How can I die? I'm booked."
—George Burns

JOKEBOOK PUBLISHER JOKES

Since jokebook publishers profit so much from jokes at other people's expense, we'll even up the score now with some jokes on them. In the interest of brevity they shall be hereinafter referred to as "JBP's."

Why don't JBP's like hunting elephants? Because they get tired of carrying the decoys.

* * * *

A JBP told a friend about an exciting vacation package that's extra-low cost and they decided to go together. When they got to the remote camp late that night, they had to sleep on the cold, stony ground near a nest of scorpions.
Awakened at dawn by a 'recreation director' with a bull whip, they were told that they were going bungee jumping, naked, from a moving helicopter.
Strapped to seats outside the chopper while it flew up high over the mountains, the pair were told to slip the bungee cords around their ankles but the cords were cracked and worn and when they jumped, the cords snapped, sending the men plummeting hundreds of feet head down into deep snowdrifts so that only their feet were sticking above the frozen landscape. The dazed friend cleared the snow from his mouth and said, "What a rotten vacation! I wonder if they'll at least come pick us up?"
And the JBP said, "Gee, I don't know. They did last year."

* * * *

Then there were the two JBP's who went deep into the frozen woods searching for a Christmas tree. After hours of sub-zero temperatures and a few close calls with hungry wolves, one JBP turned to the other and said, "I'm chopping down the next tree I see. I don't care whether it's decorated or not!"

Q: Why did the JBP return the necktie he got for Father's Day?
A: It was too tight.

✱ ✱ ✱ ✱

And of course you heard about the guy who made a fortune at a JBP's convention selling Cheerios for ten dollars apiece. He told them that they were bagel seeds.

✱ ✱ ✱ ✱

One fellow became a JBP only after failing as a pharmacist. Seems he could never get the little bottles in the typewriter.

✱ ✱ ✱ ✱

Interested in a brain transplant? A scientist's brain costs a thousand dollars. A philosopher's brain goes for five thousand and a JBP brain sells for one hundred thousand dollars—and that's a bargain because it's never been used!

✱ ✱ ✱ ✱

And then there was the JBP who was so clumsy, he even tripped over cordless phones!

✱ ✱ ✱ ✱

"A terrible thing happened to a JBP that I know."
"What's that?"
"He accidentally locked his keys in the car."
"Well, that's inconvenient, not terrible."
"Are you kidding? It took him a week to get his family out!"

Two JBP's on vacation:

JBP #1: Hey, this is sure a great spot for fishing!

JBP #2: Yeah, but how will we be sure to find it again tomorrow?

JBP #1: Easy, Dummy, just mark an "X" on the bottom of the boat.

JBP #2: Yeah, but what if we don't get the same boat?

* * * *

The next day, these same two JBP's went fishing again and the first asked the second, "Hey, what do we do if the boat springs a leak?"

"That's easy," replied his buddy. "Put a bucket under it!"

* * * *

Later that afternoon, the boat did spring a leak and the two JBP's had resorted to bailing for all they were worth.

JBP #1: Do you think that we're getting anywhere?

JBP #2: Sure. I just looked over the side and the water level outside the boat is going up!

* * * *

One day, as a vacationing JBP strolled the beautiful beach of Sanibel Island, he came upon a bejeweled lamp partially hidden under a clump of seaweed at the high tide mark. Picking up the lamp, the JBP rubbed it and lo and behold, a genie appeared.

"I am the genie of the lamp and I will grant you three wishes but be advised, whatever you ask for, I will give twice as much to every other jokebook publisher in the world."

The excited JBP finally regained his composure and said, "Oh, great genie, I wish for a million dollars!"

"It is done," said the genie and with a nod, a huge mound of cash appeared on the sand. "Just remember that I am giving every other jokebook publisher in the world TWO million dollars!"

"That's OK, but now I want a brand new Mercedes," replied the JBP.

"It is done," nodded the genie. "One Mercedes for you and two for every other jokebook publisher in the world! Now, what is your third wish, Master?"

"Well, Genie," answered the JBP. "It's like this. Right now I'd like to have you choke me half to death!"

Miss Latour, the JBP's loyal secretary, stepped into his office late one Friday afternoon with a bundle of checks.

"Now the first one here is for $85,000. That's for the new Jaguar you ordered," she said as she placed the draft in front of him to sign.

"This next one's for your wife's mink coat. It's in the amount of $15,000 and this other one for $800,000 covers the full purchase price for your new beachfront condo in Hawaii. This check for $40,000 is for your son's first semester at Harvard and this final payment of $450,000 is for your new custom-built yacht."

As the JBP dashed off his signature on all the checks, the secretary worked up her courage, cleared her throat and said, "Pardon me, Sir, but I need to talk with you. Since I haven't had a salary increase in three years, money is getting sort of tight. A twenty dollar weekly raise would really help me out."

"TWENTY DOLLARS!!!" screamed the JBP. "What do you think I am—a millionaire?"

* * * *

The JBP's Association is excited about their new million dollar lottery. Pick the right 6 numbers and you win a dollar a year for a million years!

* * * *

And finally, a JBP is walking down a street in Manhattan carrying a car door under his arm.

A cop spots him and asks him why he's carrying a car door.

"Well, that should be obvious, Officer," says the JBP. In case it gets hot, I can roll the window down!"

* * * *

A floozy and her floo-zer were walking down the street when she spotted a beautiful fur coat in a store window.

"Oooooo, I'd love that coat!" purred the young lady to her companion.

Without batting an eye, he picked up a brick, smashed the display window, retrieved the mink and draped it over her shoulders as they walked on. A short time later, they passed a jewelry store.

"Oooooo, I'd love that diamond ring," she cooed, admiring a rock not too terribly much smaller than Gibraltar. Without saying a word, her Galahad picked up a brick, smashed the window, plucked the precious stone from the debris and placed it on her dainty finger.

They walked on a short distance and as they turned a corner, she caught sight of a brand new Jaguar gleaming in a showroom window.

Putting on her sexiest voice, the glamour girl whispered, "Oooooo, I'd love that beautiful Jaguar." Her boyfriend stopped, turned around and snapped, "Hey, whaddaya think I'm made of, bricks?"

Thoughts from the Throne

"I have a great diet. You're allowed to eat anything you want, but you must eat it with naked fat people."

—Ed Bluestone

On his first day at the asylum, the new doctor was greeted by one of the facility's craziest inmates.

"Hey, Doc, it's great to have you here. We like you much better than the old shrink!"

"That's very nice to hear," beamed the flattered psychiatrist. "But why do you like me so much?"

"Because," said the wild-eyed lunatic, "you're just like one of the boys!"

One day at the Customs counter, an agent suspiciously eyed a bottle hidden in the luggage of a tourist returning from Europe.

"And what's this, Ma'am?" he asked.

"Oh, it's just a bottle of holy water from Lourdes," said the sweet little old lady.

The inspector uncapped the bottle, took one whiff and said, "Whiskey!"

"Whiskey?" cried the woman. "Glory be to the highest! Another miracle!"

* * * *

Pot Shots

One sunny day about 40 years ago, a farmer confronted his son out behind the barn.

"Elwood, was it you who pushed the outhouse down the hill?"

"No, Sir, it sure 'nuff wasn't," replied the fresh-faced lad.

"Now, Son, let me tell you a little story. Back when George Washington was a lad about your age, his father asked him if he chopped down the cherry tree and George answered, 'I cannot tell a lie. It was I who chopped down the cherry tree.' Well, Son, his pa was so impressed with his honesty that he didn't punish him at all. So let me ask you again. Was it you who rolled the outhouse down the hill?"

"I cannot tell a lie," replied Elwood. "I rolled the outhouse down the hill."

With that his father produced a hickory switch and gave the boy a first class wailing.

"But Pa," Elwood cried. "George Washington didn't get no beating when he 'fessed up to chopping down the cherry tree!"

"That's right, Son, but George Washington's pa wasn't IN the cherry tree at the time!"

From the Garden of Eden:

Eve: Do you love me, Adam?
Adam: Who else?

* * * *

A traveling preacher was way out in the sticks one day when his car broke down. The temperature was 95 degrees and he had no water so he said a prayer for help and then lifted the hood of his car.

After a minute or so of staring blankly at the engine he heard a voice say, "It's the fuel pump."

The preacher looked around and saw an old horse looking over his shoulder.

"It's the fuel pump," the horse said once again. "Don't worry, though. Old George Buckley comes this way every day around this time. You can hitch a ride with him."

The preacher spent the next few minutes thanking the Lord and the horse for the help and then, sure enough, Buckley's car came bouncing down the deserted road and good old George offered the preacher a ride into town.

Striding into the gas station, the preacher went up to the mechanic and said, "Brother, it's a miracle. I was lost and alone. My car broke down but my faith didn't. I prayed for help and it came in the form of a talking horse who told me that it was my fuel pump and that someone would come along in a few minutes to pick me up. That horse was a miracle, I tell you!"

Old Clem, the mechanic, spat out his tobacco and wiped the grease from his hands as he drawled, " 'Tain't such a miracle, Reverend. That horse talks big but he don't know nothin' 'bout engines!"

Thoughts from the Throne

"Interest your kids in bowling. Get them off the streets and into the alleys."
—Don Rickles

SERVICE WITH A SNEER

Customer: Waitress, this food isn't fit for a pig!
Waitress: Then let me take it back, Sir, and I'll get you some that is!

* * * *

Customer: Waiter, do you serve crabs here?
Waiter: Certainly, Sir, have a seat!

* * * *

Waiter: Sir, I'll have you know that we run a very clean restaurant here!
Customer: Must be—all the food tastes like soap!

* * * *

Diner: Hey Waiter, this plate is wet!
Waiter: That's your soup, Sir!

* * * *

A guy goes home with a black eye and explains to his wife that the waitress slugged him.
"Getting fresh again, huh, Henry?"
"No. I just asked the waitress if she had frog's legs!"

* * * *

Patron: Hey, Waiter, how come the white-plate special is $5 more than the blue-plate special?
Waiter: With the white-plate special, we clean the plate!

In Washington, D.C., a tourist observed two Federal workers moving along a busy street. One would dig a hole beside the road and the other would follow right behind and immediately fill it

"Excuse me," she finally interrupted. "But I can't see that you're accomplishing anything here. Would you mind explaining to a curious taxpayer exactly what you're doing?"

"Well, Ma'am," said Slim in his slow drawl. "You see we're working on the Capitol Beautification Project. Fred, here, he digs a hole; Delbert sticks a tree in the hole and I follow along behind and fill it back in."

"But there are only two of you here."

"That's right, Ma'am, but just 'cause Delbert's out sick doesn't mean that Fred and me can't work!"

* * * *

When a government report came out listing a small Arkansas town as the healthiest place in the entire country to live, the media swarmed all over the place seeking to discover its secrets.

The town's aged residents soon found themselves the center of attention and they were in great demand for interviews.

Soon there was only one old codger left to tell his tale. He astounded the press with the story that when he first came to the town, he was bald, toothless and couldn't walk. Now, he's a relatively robust 85.

"That's amazing, Sir!" exclaimed one of the reporters. Exactly when did you come here?"

"Eighty-five years ago," said the oldster with a wink. "I was born here!"

* * * *

The little boy got his first real bow and arrow for his 10th birthday and went out into the yard to practice.

A few minutes later his father stepped outside to check how he was doing and was amazed to see a dozen arrows dead in the centers of as many bullseyes painted on the trees and the backyard fence.

"That's astounding, Son. You just got that bow a few minutes ago. How do you manage to hit a bullseye every time?"

"Easy, Dad. First I shoot the arrow. Then wherever it lands, I paint circles around it!"

* * * *

Thoughts from the Throne

"I looked up the word 'politics' in the dictionary and it's actually a combination of two words; 'poli,' which means many, and 'tics,' which means bloodsuckers."

—*Jay Leno*

* * * *

The night court judge was mass-dispensing justice when he got to the case of one young fellow who pleaded guilty to robbing a liquor store.

"Have you ever been in trouble before?" asked the judge.

"Just once," replied the young man. "I once stole from my kid brother's bank."

"Well, that doesn't sound serious," said the judge.

"My brother thought it was," answered the defendant. "It cost him his job as president of the First National!"

Three pals, Farr, Smith and Away, went deep sea fishing one afternoon but didn't return to port as scheduled.

The Coast Guard snapped into action and organized a search for the trio which went on for days.

Finally, when almost all hope was gone, the rescue planes spotted two of the men clinging to wreckage which had been carried hundreds of miles by the currents. There was no trace of the third fisherman.

A rescue boat was dispatched and after they pulled Smith and Farr out of the water the Coast Guardsmen heard the pair's eerie tale.

"We were fishing about 20 miles offshore when a strange fog came up out of nowhere," said Farr.

"Yeah, and suddenly the boat began rocking violently," said Smith.

"Then a giant fire-breathing fish with long dorsal spines, purple and orange scales and teeth 12 inches long emerged from the deep and smashed the boat into kindling. We only survived by playing dead."

"Wow!" said the young Coast Guard officer. "That must have been some fish!"

"Oh, that's nothing," said one of the anglers. "You should have seen the one that got Away!"

* * * *

Late at night in a cross-country train, the woman in the upper berth leaned out and said to the man in the lower, "Excuse me, but it's awfully cold. I wonder if you could get me another blanket?"

"Tell you what, Lady," answered the stranger. "Why don't we just pretend that we're married?"

The woman flushed with embarrassment but managed a shy, "Well, I guess that would be all right."

"Good!" said her traveling companion. "Then get your own stupid blanket!!"

* * * *

Business Cards

Who says businesspeople can't be funny-businesspeople? Consider some of these signs and slogans from the world of commerce . . .

On a watch and clock repair shop: If it doesn't tick—tock to us!

* * * *

Sign outside the permanently sealed reactor at Three Mile Island: Gone Fission.

* * * *

Wintertime sign outside a Minnesota nudist camp: Clothed for the Season.

* * * *

On an obstetrician's business card: We Deliver!

* * * *

Then there's the voodoo school which advertises: Hex Education.

* * * *

Business conditions were grave for the undertaker until he hit upon a bright slogan: Count on us. We're the last ones to ever let you down!

* * * *

Of course the ladies flock to the plastic surgeon whose card reads: Droop Therapy.

* * * *

Then there's the sign on the desk of the head engraver at the U.S. Mint: The Buck Starts Here.

* * * *

One of the few companies that specializes in cleaning up nuclear waste spills calls itself: The fastest relief known for atomic ache!

* * * *

Although he never had it printed anywhere, there was the dermatologist who'd tell anyone who'd listen that he built his business from scratch.

* * * *

Speaking of doctors, two specialists, a psychiatrist and a proctologist, teamed up for a medical practice. Their business card reads: Odds and Ends.

* * * *

And finally, one movie company sued for a consultancy fee to be returned. Seems the expert P. R. man advised Miracle Pictures to use the slogan: If It's a Good Picture, It's a Miracle.

Thoughts from the Throne

"Asthma doesn't seem to bother me any more unless I'm around cigars or dogs. The thing that would bother me most would be a dog smoking a cigar. "

—*Steve Allen*

An accountant at a big income tax service could hardly stay awake at his desk and his yawns finally prompted a rebuke by his boss.

"Finster, what's wrong with you anyway? It looks like you've been burning the candle at both ends!"

"Sorry, Boss," answered the meek C.P.A. "But I had insomnia last night."

"Didn't you try counting sheep?" inquired his boss.

"Yes, Sir, I tried that but I made a mistake and then it took me all night to find it!"

❋ ❋ ❋ ❋

It was Saturday afternoon at the firehouse and the smoke eaters were sitting around playing cards when the emergency phone rang.

"Station 6, Clancy speaking," the fireman said as he picked up the receiver.

"Hurry, my house is on fire!" came the frantic voice. "You've got to come quick!"

"All right, Lady, calm down. Now how do we get there?"

"How should I know?" shrieked the caller. "Don't you have that big red truck anymore?"

Back in the days of the Wild West, two cowboys were riding from Laramie to Dodge City when they happened upon an old Indian on the trail.

The Indian was lying on his side with his ear to the ground and one cowboy said to the other, "You got to respect these Indians. When they do that they can tell what's coming for miles in all directions."

As the cowboys passed close to the Indian, they heard him say in a low voice, "Stagecoach, loaded with gold for Fort Wilson, 6 horses in team, 1 broken spoke in left rear wheel, driver red-haired with bushy moustache."

One of the cowboys, beaming with admiration, said, "Wow! You can tell all that just from the vibrations in the ground?"

"No," said the Indian. "It run me over half-hour ago!"

* * * *

A disheveled young fellow shambled into the office of a car agency's sales manager.

He took one look at the manager and mumbled, "I guess you don't want to buy any life insurance," and he turned to walk away.

"Hold on, Son!" called the sales manager. "I've been in sales for 40 years and I have to say that I have never seen a worse sales approach. But I like you, Boy, and I'm going to help, sort of take you under my wing so to speak. The first thing you've got to do is gain confidence and to help you out, I want you to write me up for a $100,000 policy."

As soon as the insurance novice had his signature on the dotted line, he began to leave but the manager called him back. "Hold on, Son. Now that you've got confidence, you've got to learn the tricks of the trade."

"Oh, yes, Sir, the tricks of the trade are very important," replied the young insurance agent. "The one I just used on you is designed especially for sales managers!"

* * * *

Q: What do you get if you cross a dog with a chicken?
A: Pooched eggs.

Thoughts from the Throne

"The reason lightning doesn't strike twice in the same place is that the same place isn't there the second time."

—Willie Tyler

One day, at the water hole, an elephant happened to notice a snapping turtle sunning itself on a rock.

Without provocation, the elephant went over to the snapper, picked it up with his trunk and threw it through the air over the trees.

A hippo, standing nearby said, "Hey, why'd you do that? That turtle was minding its own business."

"Well," replied the elephant. "I was drinking water and I happened to remember that same snapper took a chunk out of my trunk 50 years ago."

"Man! What a memory!" exclaimed the amazed hippo.

"All elephants have it," replied the pachyderm modestly. "It's called 'turtle recall'."

＊　＊　＊　＊

An old fellow was causing quite a commotion at the movie theater.

"Listen, you," said the usher in an angry whisper. "Why are you crawling around on the floor disturbing everyone?"

"I'm looking for a caramel."

"You're causing this much trouble over a caramel?"

"It's not just any caramel. It has my teeth in it!"

＊　＊　＊　＊

Parrots live a long time, often surviving their owners. And so it was with Clancy, the beloved companion of the late Big Mike Gilhooly, the roughest, toughest sailor who ever sailed the seven seas.

Now being a sailor's companion as he was, Clancy picked up some salty language. In fact, there wasn't a socially unacceptable word that he didn't know and use with relish.

Since Gilhooly had no heirs, none that would own up to it anyway, Clancy wound up in a pet shop. One day a sweet little old lady came in and fell in love with the beautiful parrot. The owner tried to warn her but her mind was made up and she took the bird home.

No sooner had she hung the cage up in the living room than Clancy piped up with, "Shiver me timbers, Lady, you're as ugly as a %$#@*&%!!! garbage scow!"

Well, to curtail his propensity for colorful language, she put the bird in the freezer for a few minutes to let him reconsider and it seemed to work. For the next few days he was on his best behavior.

Old habits die hard though, and one day as she was snacking on crackers, the parrot gave out with, "Hey Lady, how about some of them %$#@*&%$!! crackers?"

The parrot was back in the freezer faster than he knew what hit him and the ordeal cooled his enthusiasm for vulgarity for several weeks.

One day near Thanksgiving though, Clancy opened his big beak again and got the bum's rush to the freezer compartment once more. As he was thrown in the freezer he happened to see a 15 pound Butterball, all plucked, cleaned and frozen stiff. Clancy got a horrified look on his face and squawked, "Holy smoke, Buddy! What the $%#@!!&! did you say?"

* * * *

Woman: I want you to tell my future.
Fortune Teller: You will meet a tall, dark, handsome stranger...
Woman: Go on.
Fortune Teller: He will sweep you off your feet and you will fall madly in love!
Woman: Go on!
Fortune Teller: He is very wealthy and will take you away to live in his castle on a beautiful island off the south of France.
Woman: Great! Just one question?
Fortune Teller: What's that?
Woman: What are we going to do about my husband?

Two auto dealers discussing the recession were trying to one-up each other about how bad business was.

"I tell you, George, business is terrible. I only sold one car yesterday."

"Oh, yeah?" retorted George. "Well, I also only sold one car yesterday and today it's even worse!"

"Geez, how could it be worse than that?" asked Charlie.

"Well, today," answered George, "the customer returned it!"

✹ ✹ ✹ ✹

Tenant: I want to make a complaint about my upstairs neighbors. Last night they were shouting and banging on the floor until all hours of the night!

Landlord: I'm sorry. Did they wake you up?

Tenant: No. Fortunately, I was up late practicing on my tuba.

Thoughts from the Throne

"I talk to myself because I like dealing with a better class of people."

—Jackie Mason

✹ ✹ ✹ ✹

A city slicker was driving through the country when he spotted a horse standing in a field. He was quite taken with the animal and so pulled over to ask the farmer if it was for sale.

"Afraid not," said the farmer.

"I'll give you a thousand bucks!" said the city fella.

"I can't sell that horse. He don't look too good," replied the farmer.

"I know horses and he looks fine. I'll give you two thousand!"

"Well, all right, if you want him so bad."

The next day, the man returned with the horse, screaming that he had been gypped. "You sold me a blind horse!"

"Well," said the farmer, "I told you he didn't look too good."

During World War II a French farmer was standing out in his field by a huge ditch yelling, "43! 43! 43!"

A passing Nazi officer walked up to the peasant and demanded to know what he was doing.

The farmer just kept repeating, "43! 43! 43!" and pointed to the ditch.

The officious Nazi commander goose stepped over to the edge and peered down into the ditch. Just as he did, the farmer smacked him on the head with a shovel, pushed him in the ditch and began yelling, "44! 44! 44!"

Thoughts from the Throne

"I don't think anybody should write his autobiography until after he's dead."
—*Samuel Goldwyn*

A wealthy woman, moved by her minister's sermon to do something for the needy, scribbled 'Best of Luck' on a $100 bill and went downtown to give it to the first poor person she met.

While walking down the street, she spotted a suitably seedy-looking fellow and as she passed him, she pressed the bill into his hand.

The next day, she returned to the street to see if the money did the fellow any good. She caught sight of him once again and as she approached, he pressed $1000 into her hand and said, "Nice bet, Lady. Best of Luck paid 10 to 1!"

✳ ✳ ✳ ✳

A guy goes into the psychiatrist's office, takes a seat and says, "Doc, my memory's terrible. I can't remember anything from one minute to the next!"

"I see," says the shrink, scratching his chin. "And how long has this been going on?"

"How long has what been going on?"

PUN-ZZLES

Here are some real groaners with everything but the PUNch line included. From the tortuous twists and turns of the set-up, you should be able to figure out the pun. Think of it as a mini-mystery with wordplay instead of foulplay . . .

#1—20 points

The hotel manager was grumbling, "Bah! Humbug!" under his breath and his assistant asked him what was wrong.

"I hate Christmas," the manager growled. "Every year we get the annual holiday convention of Chessmasters at our hotel. These guys are obsessed. All these guys do, for days on end, is stand around in the hall by the main entrance bragging about their conquests and checkmates on the board!"

Suddenly his assistant brightened and said, "Oh, you mean it's just like that Christmas tune . . . .

#2—20 points

One day at the zoo, a workman happened to leave a stack of tiles in the gnu enclosure. He was surprised the next morning to find that all the tiles had been perfectly laid down. He did the same thing at quitting time once again and found the tiles all perfectly inlaid by the next morning. Astonished, he ran to the zookeeper with the news but the man wasn't impressed. "Oh, it's nothing that unusual," he yawned. "You see the animal is . . . .

#3—20 points

Then there was the photographer who heard a legend that in a certain Scottish castle a ghost appeared at the stroke of midnight on the first day of each new decade. Having just barely enough time to get there, he gathered up his gear and caught the first flight out. He made it to the castle just as the clock was striking twelve and, sure enough, there was the ghost. He snapped in a new bulb for the flash and the ghost posed as he snapped off a shot. The bulb, however, was defective and just sort of fizzled. He was bitterly disappointed but held out hope until the next day when the picture came back totally blank. "I suppose I should be philosophical," the photographer said. "This is just another case where . . . .

And finally, here's #4, a 40 pointer . . .

And speaking of photographers, famed shutterbug, Matthew Brady, one of the founding fathers of the art, produced a stunning photographic record of the Civil War. Naturally with much of his work involving the military, discretion was essential and he had to be on good terms with officers wearing both the blue and the gray. And so it was until a Confederate colonel saw Brady in a cape and had him thrown in the stockade for spying. When asked why he did, the colonel said, "Oh, that photographer you know his kind. In espionage we'd call him a real

. . . .   (Answers on next page)

The Bathroom Joke Book

Pun-zzles Answers

#1. "Chess nuts boasting by an open foyer . . ."

#2. ". . . typical gnu and tiler too."

#3. ". . . the spirit was willing but the flash was weak."

#4. ". . . cloak and daguerrotype."

Scoring

0-20 Chinese food on sacred Indian wood carving. (Lo Mein on the Totem Pole).

20-40 You're like a general in command of the clerical pool. (You're among the rank and file).

40-60 Acupuncturist. (A jab well done).

60-plus You're like the top students at the Barber College. (At the head of the class).

* * * *

Billionaire H. Ross Perot attended an art auction in New York and snapped up 2 Van Goghs, 4 Rembrandts, 2 Da Vincis, 7 Picassos and a dozen assorted Monets and Gauguins.

On his way out, a frustrated art dealer who had been outbid on every one of the masterpieces asked him, "What are you doing, Mr. Perot, starting your own museum?"

"Nah," said the rich Texan, "just shopping for Christmas cards."

* * * *

A salesman was in the habit of scratching important numbers on small pieces of paper and sticking them in his suit pockets. Naturally, when the suits went out to be cleaned, his wife saved the tiny bits of paper.

Finally, one weekend she cornered him and said, "Frank, you have got a whole shoebox full of phone numbers on our dresser. Here's a phone book I bought you. Copy all those numbers down and let's get rid of the slips!"

Frank spent most of the afternoon filing the names and numbers in his new book but there were about a half-dozen that he couldn't identify. These might be important sales contacts, he thought, so on Monday he'd make a point of calling them.

On his first call on Monday, he cheerily dialed an unidentified number and said, "Hi! This is Frank Sheffield of Metro Meats. I'm just calling to remind you that if there's anything that I can ever do for you, just ask."

"Well, thanks a lot, Frank," came the voice over the phone. "But you've already done more for me than you'll ever know. This is your wife's first husband!"

* * * *

A little boy goes up to his dad who is sitting in his easy chair reading the paper.

"Dad," says the tyke, "why is the sky blue?"

"Gee, Son, I don't know," came his father's reply.

"Dad, how come there's that extra 'd' in Wednesday?"

"Gee, Son, I don't know."

"Dad, how come people drive on parkways but park on driveways?"

"Gee, Son, I don't know."

"Dad, do you mind me asking you all these questions?"

"Of course not, Son. How else would you ever learn anything?"

Thoughts from the Throne

"I'm sure George Washington, the father of our country, would be proud to know that we celebrate his birthday every year with a mattress sale."
—Robert Klein

HAIR-BRAINED HUMOR

One of the biggest joke crazes of all time is the "blonde" joke. The term "dumb blonde" conjures up images of bleached bimbo bombshells, but fair-haired folks are really no different from anyone else with the possible exception that they have more fun.

With that in mind, let's recast these jokes so that they fit people of any hair color, length, texture or origin, natural or artificial. We'll call them hair-brains, those people that we all know whose roots obviously go WAY too deep . . .

Q: If you push a bald man and a hair-brained man off the Empire State Building, which one will hit the ground first?

A: The bald man. The hair-brained man has to stop to ask directions.

❋ ❋ ❋ ❋

Q: What goes vrrrooooom-screech, vrrrooooom-screech, vrrrooooomscreech?

A: A hair-brained sports car driver trying to get through a flashing red light.

❋ ❋ ❋ ❋

Q: What's a hair-brained guy doing when he grasps at thin air?
A: Collecting his thoughts.

❋ ❋ ❋ ❋

Q: Why do many hair-brains wear their hair in pony tails?
A: To cover the valve stem.

❋ ❋ ❋ ❋

Q: Why don't hair-brains like to make Kool-Aid?
A: They have a hard time getting all that water in the package.

* * * *

Q: Why shouldn't hair-brains take coffee breaks?
A: Because it takes too long to retrain them.

* * * *

Q: Why did the hair-brain want to become a plastic surgeon?
A: He yearned to repair Tupperware.

* * * *

Q: Why don't hair-brains eat pickles?
A: Because they can't get their heads in the jar.

* * * *

Q: Where will a hair-brain look if you say, "There's a dead bird?"
A: Up in the air.

* * * *

Q: What's the first thing hair-brains do if they see a sign that says 'Clean Restrooms Ahead'?
A: Reach for the Lysol.

* * * *

Q: How does a hair-brain play hookey at correspondence school?
A: Sends in empty envelopes.

✳ ✳ ✳ ✳

First Guy at Bar: My wife and I had another terrible argument.

Second Guy at Bar: Oh yeah? How did it come out?

First Guy at Bar: The usual. She came crawling to me on her hands and knees.

Second Guy at Bar: Really? What'd she say?

First Guy at Bar: She said, "Come out from under that bed, you miserable weasel, and fight like a man!

Pot Shots

Finster loved all the latest gadgets and so when the musical toilet seat came out he just had to have one. One day his wife's bridge club was at his house and the ladies took turns using the facilities.

The first lady came back all a—twitter and a-gog. "Oh, what a surprise! A musical toilet seat! Can you imagine that? It played 'Stardust' for me!"

A few minutes later, another woman returned to the living room and reported that it played Beethoven's Fifth Symphony!

The latest in bathroom appliances was a huge hit as one by one, all the ladies tried it out.

Finally, it was Shirley's turn but she returned from the john none-too-pleased.

"What's wrong, Dear? Didn't you like it?", asked a concerned Mrs. Finster.

"It's all right, I guess," answered Shirley hesitantly. "It's just that not only did I have to wait till last to use the bathroom, but as soon as I sit down it starts playing 'The Star Spangled Banner'!"

In the days when Buccaneers ruled the Spanish Main, one member of a pirate crew was captured by a rival group of plunderers.

"Aye," said the captain, "he was a member of Blackbeard's crew. He knows where the great treasure is buried."

"But there's a problem, Captain," said the first mate. "He speaks a rare West Indian dialect. We can't question him if we can't understand him."

"Well, we'll stage a little night raid in Port Royal. There's a professor there who knows every language in the world."

The pirates kidnapped the professor, promising him his life in return for cooperation. Wasting no time, the interrogation began by the light of a full moon.

The captain hissed, "Tell him if he doesn't tell us where the treasure's hidden we'll tie him to the mast and give him a thousand lashes!"

The professor translated and the prisoner replied in his native babble.

"He says he'd rather die than tell you where the treasure is."

Sure enough, the prisoner was lashed to within an inch of his life.

"Now tell him if he doesn't tell us where the treasure is, we'll cut off all his fingers!" the captain growled.

The threat was translated and the reply once again was in the negative.

"He says he'd rather die than tell you where the treasure is."

The captain drew his scabbard and performed elective surgery until the prisoner's hands were fingerless stumps.

The captain now brought out the heavy artillery. "Say to him if he doesn't tell us where the treasure is, we'll dangle him by a rope and let the sharks tear him apart, appendage by appendage."

The professor translated and this time the threat struck a nerve. The prisoner babbled on saying not only where the treasure was hidden but warning of all the booby traps protecting it and supplying an entire inventory of the gold and jewels as well as offering to guide the captain there, personally.

"Now what did he say to that, Professor?" snarled the pirate captain.

"Poor devil," sighed the professor. "He said he'd rather die than tell you where the treasure is . . ."

* * * *

Thoughts from the Throne

"They should put expiration dates on clothes so we would know when they go out of style."
—*Garry Shandling*

Driving along a deserted country road late one night, Steve noticed a car with a flat tire pulled over on the shoulder. Behind the car stood a rather perplexed, pretty and petite young lady.

Since he considered himself the Keeper of the Flame of Chivalry, Steve pulled over and without a word rolled up his sleeves and set to work changing the flat. It was quite a struggle with the car in soft mud and the lug nuts rusted on, but he finally managed it although it left him a greasy mess.

As he was about to put the tools away, the young woman spoke up.

"Thank you so much, but I have one more favor to ask of you. Please let the car down off the jack very gently. My husband's asleep in the back seat!"

❋   ❋   ❋   ❋

"Son," said the old man passing control of the family business to his eldest boy. "The most important things in business are integrity and wisdom."

"How do you define integrity, Dad?" asked the young man.

"Integrity, my boy, is keeping your promises to the customers even if it means losing money."

"And what is wisdom?"

"Wisdom is knowing enough not to make those stupid promises in the first place!"

❋   ❋   ❋   ❋

At an Atlantic City nightspot, the manager called his headliner, The Great Curreri, into his office. He complained to the hypnotist, "When you first started here last summer, the people you put under would stay in the trance for quite a while, but ever since Labor Day, you seem to have trouble keeping them hypnotized. What's the trouble?"

"Well, Boss," replied Curreri. "Now that autumn's here, you have to expect that the daze will be shorter!"

* * * *

Mrs Frobush was called into school to meet with the principal about her son's behavior.

"Mrs. Frobush," began the principal. "Your son is a very high-spirited boy. In the past two weeks alone, he's broken three windows, set all the frogs and snakes in the biology lab free, gotten caught smoking in the boy's room five times, was late for class twelve times and snuck into the girl's shower room. As I said, he's very high-spirited, but I wish that I had a hundred like him."

Mrs. Frobush looked surprised. "My, if he's all that much trouble, why do you wish you had a hundred like him?"

"Because right now," the principal sighed, "I've got a THOUSAND like him!"

* * * *

Thoughts from the Throne

"Why is there always a mailbox in front of the post office?"

—*Gallagher*

* * * *

Then there was the old minister who wanted to see the Grand Canyon on horseback. He got there late in the day, however, and the stables had only one horse left.

"I feel I have to warn you about this horse, Reverend," said the man as he saddled up the steed. "His name's Zealot and he's a bit odd but completely controllable if you know the right commands. Now if you want him to giddyup, you have to say, "Praise the Lord!" When you want him to stop, say, "Amen!"

Feeling confident about such terminology, the minister rented the steed and climbed into the saddle. "Praise the Lord!" intoned the old Reverend and the horse took off at a full gallop. The tenderfoot minister was terrified at the speed and, what was worse, the horse was heading right for the edge of the canyon.

In his desperate and panicky state, the stop command had completely gone out of the minister's head and so he started shouting every religious and biblical term he could think of.

"Hallelujah!" "Repent!" "Sermon!" "Fire and Brimstone!" "Pass the plate!" Nothing worked. At last, when he was only two feet from the precipice, divine inspiration hit. "AMEN!" he shouted at the top of his lungs and the runaway horse screeched to a halt at the very edge of the cliff. The minister, quite shook up, mopped his brow, gazed down into the rocky chasm a full mile deep and, grateful for his deliverance, looked up and said with a sigh of relief, "Praise the Lord!"

✻ ✻ ✻ ✻

Pot Shots

A psychiatrist was handed a $150 bill by his plumber for fixing a faucet washer. Indignantly the doctor said, "You didn't spend ten minutes on that. I'm a psychiatrist and even I don't make that kind of money!"

"I know," said the plumber. "When I was a psychiatrist, neither did I!"

The battle had been raging in the divorce court and it was time for the wife to testify.

"He drives me crazy, You Honor," the woman sobbed. "Horseracing! That's all he ever thinks about—horseracing. Morning, noon and night, horseracing was all he ever really cared about. He knew all about the ponies but he couldn't even remember our wedding anniversary."

"That's a lie!" yelled the husband jumping to his feet. "I remember the date well. We were married the day Secretariat won the Kentucky Derby!"

※　※　※　※

Zeb, a downeaster farmer working the rocky fields of Maine, hated to part with the money but there had recently been a spate of severe storms whipping up the coast and so, for his family's safety, he grudgingly agreed to build a storm shelter.

The next hurricane that approached, Zeb herded his family underground and sat out the storm. When they emerged, Zeb was disgusted. There was hardly any damage at all. The money for the storm shelter had been wasted.

This went on, season after season. The family hid out in the storm shelter but when they emerged, there was very little damage anyway.

One day, during a full moon high tide, a monster hurricane approached. The winds were 150 mph and, once again, Zeb and the family took shelter in the bunker. This time when they came out, they were faced with a scene of total devastation. The crops were gone; the fields were a mass of mud; the farmhouse was smashed to kindling wood and the barn was nowhere to be found.

"At last!" said Zeb brightening. "I finally got my money's worth!"

※　※　※　※

ADULT RIDDLES

Q: What's 10-9-8-7-6-5-4-3-2-1?
A: Bo Derek getting older.

Q: What's 1-2-3-4-5-6-7-8-9-10?
A: The girl sitting next to you at the singles bar as closing time approaches.

＊ ＊ ＊ ＊

Deadbeat Dave went through life mooching off people and racking up bills that he never intended to pay. He had gone bankrupt several times already and his lawyer warned him that he couldn't use that as an out anymore.

"What am I gonna do?" fretted Dave. "I'm into a lot of people for big money. Some of these people are pretty tough. How am I gonna squirm out of this one?"

"Well," said the lawyer, "it's pretty drastic but I've seen it work before. We make out like you died, see? We stage a mock funeral, with you laid out and everything and your creditors come by, see that you're dead and just write off their money."

Dave agreed and within a few weeks everything was set. His lawyer had even managed to rent a coffin.

Sure enough, all the people Dave owed money to filed past the coffin just to be sure that he was really dead.

"Poor Dave," said one. "He stiffed me for a thousand bucks but I'm sorry to see him go so young."

"Yeah, it's a real shame," said another mourner. "He was into me for five thousand, but what's money at a time like this?"

This went on and on until, near the end of the service, a man with a beet-red face approached the casket.

"You dirty deadbeat!" he screamed. "You think that you can run up a twenty thousand dollar bill with me and get out of it just by dying! You louse!! You creep! Well, at least I'm going to get some satisfaction out of this." With that, he pulled a 357 Magnum from his coat and took aim at Dave.

Suddenly the corpse sat up, motioned for the man to calm down, and said, "Take it easy. YOU, I'll pay!"

Q: What do dentists take to cure a toothache?
A: About fifty bucks.

* * * *

Little Billy: Hey, Mom, would you ever punish me for something I didn't do?
Mom: Of course not.
Little Billy: Good, because I didn't do my homework.

* * * *

IRS Auditor: I've got good news and bad news, Mr. Philby.
Taxpayer: What's the bad news?
IRS Auditor: We haven't yet finished auditing your returns.
Taxpayer: So what's the good news?
IRS Auditor: We've seen enough to be interested in buying the fiction rights.

* * * *

Confucious say: Business of man who bet too much on football, often wind up in hands of receiver.

* * * *

Thoughts from the Throne

"I go for two kinds of men.
Foreign and domestic."
—Mae West

MARTIAN JOKES

A Martian approached a gas pump and asked directions to Washington, D.C. The alien repeated himself over and over but, of course, got no response. As the alien was climbing back into his saucer, his co-pilot asked, "Well, did you find out anything?"

"Nah," said the first Martian. "The idiot just stood there with his finger in his ear the whole time!"

* * * *

Two Martians walk through an Atlantic City casino. Just as they pass the dollar slot machines, a one-armed bandit starts ringing, flashing and spewing out mounds of silver dollars.

One Martian turns to the other and says, "You know, he really should be home in bed with a cold like that!"

* * * *

A Martian landed near a roadside rest stop and wandered into the men's room. He took one look at the towel rack and said, "Pardon me, Ma'am, but your slip is showing."

* * * *

A three inch tall Martian gets out of his spaceship, goes up to Wilt Chamberlain, takes one look at the seven footer and says, "Take me to your ladder!"

* * * *

A Martian goes up to an IBM mainframe, gives a whistle and says, "Hey, Babe, how about a little computer dating?"

A Martian making his way through Lower Manhattan is approached by a panhandler.

"Excuse me, Mister, can you spare a quarter?"

"What's a quarter?" the Martian asks.

"You're right, Pal," says the bum, "make it a buck!"

Thoughts from the Throne

"Never go to a doctor whose office plants have died."

—*Erma Bombeck*

Two hillbillies are sittin' under the old apple tree soakin' up some shade: Caleb: By cracky! I sure wish I had my wife back! Jethro: She left you, huh? Caleb: Not rightly. I traded her for a gallon jug of Ozark Lightning. Jethro: And now you miss her, right? Caleb: Darn tootin'! I'm thirsty again!

* * * *

A guy goes into one of those 'glasses while you wait' places and orders a new pair of specs.

"Okay, come back Thursday," said the clerk.

"But your sign says 'glasses while you wait'!" protested the customer.

"Well, you'll still be waiting, won't you?"

* * * *

Slightly sloshed guest: Pardon me, but does a lemon have wings?

Hostess: I think not.

Guest: Then, Madam, I regret to inform you that I have just squeezed your canary into my martini.

Sonny Bono went to his longtime barber and said, "Today, be sure you do an extra good job this time. Tomorrow, I'm leaving for England."

"Oh, yeah? What airline you takin'?" asked Tony as he snipped away.

"Royal Air," said Sonny.

"Oh, that's a lousy airline—awful food, awful service. So where you stayin'?"

"At the King's Arms in London."

"Geez, what a dump! You won't like it there at all! By the way, why are you going?"

"The Queen wants to honor me for my contributions to music in a private ceremony."

"Private, ha! I've heard about those things. When you show up every songwriting hack in the world will be there and the Queen will probably just wave at you from the next room!"

A few weeks later, Bono goes back to the barber and Tony says, "Hey, Sonny. How was that airline?"

"Excellent," replied Bono. "On time, fine food, courteous service . . ."

"Yeah, but that hotel was a dump, huh?"

"Not at all. It was luxurious and had a beautiful view of Big Ben."

"Well, then you really didn't get to meet the Queen in person, did you?"

"I sure did, Tony. She was on her throne when she received me and I'll never forget what she said as she bent down and whispered in my ear."

"Oh yeah? And what was that?"

"She said, 'Sonny, where'd you get that lousy haircut?' "

* * * *

Pot Shots

BATHROOM TIP: Water Conservation—remember, a small drip can waste a hundred gallons of water a day . . . so if you're that person, cut it out!!!

Bank customer: I need a two hundred dollar loan.
Loan officer: That might be arranged, but we need collateral. Do you own a car?
Bank customer: Oh, certainly, I have several. A Porsche, a Jaguar and a Rolls Royce.
Loan officer: How about a house?
Bank customer: Oh yes. I have a townhouse and an estate in the country as well as several condos in Florida.
Loan officer: And what about stocks?
Bank customer: Stocks, bonds, securities of all types.
Loan officer: Oh, come on! You must be joking!
Bank customer: Well, you started it!

* * * *

Whacker went in to see the boss about a raise and after stating his case the executive replied, "Well, Whacker, at this time, given the surfeit of qualified personnel for your position in the employment marketplace and factoring in the termination of certain governmental tax abatement policies towards our industry as well as the highly variable fiscal projections for the third quarter and allowing for your own professional performance profile, it would prove injudicious for any officer of this firm to commit to either a salary increment or to any enhancement of a personal benefits package."
Whacker was lost. "Huh? I don't get it," he said.
"Exactly," replied the boss.

* * * *

An older fellow, obviously enjoying his second childhood, was browsing through the toy shop playing with every single toy on display. Finally, he settled on a remote control plane. It took off, retracted its landing gear, had authentic insignias and lights and, if it happened to run out of fuel, the little toy crewmen could parachute to safety.
"This is a great toy!" said the clerk as he wrapped it up. "Your grandson should love it!"
"You know you're right," said the old man. "I'd better take two!"

One sweltering summer day, two ditch diggers on a road crew happened to notice that the foreman was sitting in the shade of a big old oak tree, sipping an iced tea.

"How come he gets to sit up there and we have to sweat down here?" asked one of the diggers

"I don't know," said the other. "I'll go ask him."

So the laborer climbed out of the ditch, walked over to his boss and asked, "How come we're breaking our backs in hundred degree heat and you're sitting around with a cool drink?"

"Easy," said the boss. "It's because I'm smart and you're dumb. Here, let me prove it to you." With that the boss put his hand up against the tree and said, "Go ahead, punch it. Hit it as hard as you can."

The laborer wound up with a mighty punch and swung but just before his fist made contact, the boss pulled his hand away and the guy smacked the mighty oak breaking a few knuckles in the process.

"Now get back down into the ditch where you belong!" ordered the boss.

As he climbed back down his buddy asked him what the boss said.

"He said we're down here because he's smart and we're dumb."

"What's he mean by that?" asked the second laborer.

"Here, let me show you," said the first ditchdigger, holding his hand up in front of his face. "Hit my hand as hard as you can!"

✳ ✳ ✳ ✳

The quick thinking award goes to the husband who was greeted at the door by his angry wife who chided him for forgetting her birthday.

"But, dear," he implored. "How can you expect me to remember your birthday when you never look any older?"

Thoughts from the Throne

"I won't tell you how much I weigh, but don't ever get in an elevator with me unless you're going down."
—Jack E. Leonard

Divine Madness

You could die laughing at the following collection of heavenly jokes set at the Pearly Gates . . . .

A terrible hurricane had slammed into the Mississippi Delta and the water started to rise. A devoutly religious lady scrambled up on her roof and said a prayer for deliverance. Suddenly a boat appeared and the man in it said, "Jump in, I'll take you to the shelter on high ground."

"No, thank you," the woman replied. "The Lord will provide."

The water kept rising and a few minutes later another boater showed up and offered to take her to safety.

"No, thanks, the Lord will provide," she said once more and went back to her praying.

As the tornados tore away at homes on all sides, another boat pulled up. "Lady, this is your last chance. Those twisters are heading this way and the water's almost up to your roof!"

He was dismissed as well. "The Lord will provide."

As the boat sped away, a tornado veered towards her. Everything was a swirl, a blur and then went black. The next thing she knew she was at the Pearly Gates and God was waiting for her there. She was very angry and said, "Dear God, I had faith in you and you let me down!"

To which God replied, "Let you down? What do you mean, let you down? I sent three boats!"

* * * *

On a street corner in New York a vendor waved a bouquet at a passerby. "Take home a bundle for your wife, Sir."

The passerby replied, "I'm not married."

"Then take a bundle for your sweetheart."

"I don't have a girlfriend, either."

"Well, then, take home a couple of bundles to celebrate!"

Harry the Complainer and his wife happen to pass away on the same day and as they await their interview with St. Peter at the Pearly Gates, they're approached by an angel.

"Hello," says the angel in a voice that sounds like Don Pardo. "I'm your host, Lyle, and welcome to Heaven World. In a few moments you'll be entering through our famous Pearly Gates for the most exciting adventure of your afterlife. Your admission coupon entitles you to chauffeur-driven limousine service anywhere in the universe, plus deluxe accommodations at our luxury hotel with all amenities—pool, jacuzzi, indoor tennis courts, private trainers and more. Then after your day of fun and relaxation, dine at any of our 5-star restaurants savoring the finest of every cuisine known to man "

At this point, Harry gives his wife a shove in the ribs with his elbow.

"What did you do that for?" she cries.

"If it wasn't for you and that stupid oat bran, we'd have been here ten years ago!"

A woman went into a neighborhood bakery and said to the proprietor, "Gustav, I simply must have a chocolate devil's food cake baked in the shape of an elephant."

"Okay, Ma'am," said the baker. "But that's a specialty job and it'll take three days."

"Splendid!" said the woman as she left. "I'll see you then."

Three days later, she showed up at the shop and asked for her cake.

"Here it is, by yimminy!" said the proud Gustav, presenting the cake.

The woman's face fell. "Oh, I'm afraid there's been a terrible mistake. This is an African elephant. Look at the huge ears. Did I neglect to mention that the cake has to be in the shape of an Indian elephant?"

"That's okay, Ma'am," said Gustav. It was a strange order indeed, but he believed that the customer is always right. "I'll try again and, this time, it'll be an Indian elephant for sure, but remember that it'll take three days."

Three days later the woman returned to the shop and Gustav proudly unveiled a chocolate devil's food, Indian elephant-shaped cake perfect in every detail.

"Oh, that's wonderful!" squealed the woman in delight.

"Fine, I'm glad you like it. Now should I wrap it up?"

"No, thanks," said the customer, "I'll eat it here!"

Psychiatrist: Here's a prescription for some medicine that should cure your kleptomania.
Patient: What should I do if it doesn't work?
Psychiatrist: Try to get me a VCR.

❊ ❊ ❊ ❊

Meanwhile, across town at another psychiatrist's office . . .
Patient: Doctor, you've got to help me. I think I have kleptomania. What should I do?
Shrink: Take something for it.

Thoughts from the Throne

"Have you ever noticed what golf spells backwards?"

—*Al Boliska*

❊ ❊ ❊ ❊

The old medicine man was holding a group of dude ranch guests entranced with tales of the Old West.
"Greatest brave of all was Cherokee named Shortcake. A great grizzly bear had been attacking members of his tribe and so Shortcake went into forest alone to hunt the killer. Three days and three nights passed before rescue party found Shortcake and the bear. They had died battling each other. Shortcake was hero and so they brought his body back to his wife."
"Gee, Mister Medicine Man," gushed a pimply faced rough rider from the badlands of Long Island, "whatever happened then?"
"Easy, Kid," smiled the old one, knowing the hook was set. "Squaw bury Shortcake."

"How do you get such great salespeople?" asked one company manager of another at a convention.

"Easy," replied his colleague. "It's our salesmanship training program."

"How's it work?"

"We send our trainees out to try to rent an apartment. Once they manage to get a place, we put them in the field."

"So how does that make them a good salesperson?"

"When they knock on the door to talk to the landlords, they're carrying a tuba."

* * * *

One day things were slow at the Medicine Hut and the witch doctor was catching a snooze. He awoke with a start to see a huge lion standing over him.

"Don't be afraid," said the lion. "I'm not here to eat you. I seek your advice on a professional level."

"Very well," said the witch doctor, "what can I do for you?"

"Well, Doc, it's like this. A flock of tiny birds has taken up residence in my mane. They chirp and twitter all night and I can't get any sleep. Besides, all my prey hear me coming a mile away. I've tried everything to get rid of them. Is there anything you can do?"

"Certainly," said the witch doctor. "These birds are repelled by yeast. I'll give you a good dusting and the birds will abandon their nest."

Sure enough, the next day the lion was back. "It's amazing, Doc! It was just like you said. The birds took off and my fur has been quiet ever since. Where'd you ever learn a trick like that?"

"Oh, it's really no trick," said the witch doctor modestly. "Everyone knows that yeast is yeast and nest is nest and never the mane shall tweet."

Thoughts from the Throne

"Early to bed, early to rise, and your girl goes out with other guys."

—Bob Collins

A truant officer noticed a boy of about third-grade age playing in a front yard during school hours.

"Tell me, Son, is your mother at home?"

"She sure is, Sir," was the boy's polite reply.

The truant officer rapped on the door but there was no answer. He rapped again, waited and knocked once more. Still no answer.

He pressed the door bell and waited, all the while watching the boy play away.

Finally, the truant officer walked completely around the house, tapping on all the windows and calling for the boy's mother but there was still no answer.

After 15 minutes, the exasperated truant officer said to the boy, "Son, are you absolutely sure that your mother is at home?"

"Yep, I sure am, Mister."

"Then why doesn't she answer the door?"

" 'Cause this isn't our house!"

* * * *

Pot Shots

On a dark lonely stretch of highway, a station wagon full of nuns coasted to a stop, out of gas. The youngest nun, a healthy young nurse, volunteered to set out in search of fuel but the only container that could be found that would hold gas was an old bedpan. The nun placed it under her arm and set out down the road. An hour later, her prayers were answered. There was an all night gas station.

She managed to squeeze a gallon or so into the bedpan and returned to her companions. They rigged a makeshift funnel and just as the nun was pouring the gasoline from the bedpan into the tank, a police car pulled up alongside.

Taking one look at the situation, the cop rolled down the window and said to the nun, "Sister" now THAT'S what I call Faith!"

RIMSHOTS

A man told his psychiatrist that he suspected that he had a split personality so the doctor charged him double!

* * * *

The psychiatrist told his new patient, "Since I haven't seen you before, I have no idea what your problem is so just start at the beginning." And the patient said, "Okay, Doc, in the beginning, I created Heaven and Earth . . ."

* * * *

And then there was the cheap counterfeiter. He was so tight, he had the first dollar he ever printed.

* * * *

Talk about a cheap date! His idea of a royal evening was dinner at Burger King and dessert at Dairy Queen!

* * * *

My insurance salesman set me up with a retirement policy. If I make the payments faithfully for 20 years, he can retire!

* * * *

Two fleas are coming out of Sardi's in New York on a brisk autumn evening. One flea takes a deep breath of the bracing night air and says, "Well, what do you think? Should we walk or take a dog?"

Did you hear about the big accident downtown? A cement mixer collided with a paddy wagon and the convicts escaped. That was this afternoon. Tonight the cops are looking for 10 hardened criminals.

* * * *

Q: What do you get if you cross the Gulf of Alaska with the Exxon Valdez?
A: About halfway.

* * * *

My ex-wife and her new husband are a fastidious couple. She's fast and he's hideous!

* * * *

It's hard to get good help nowadays. The new elevator operator in my building was fired because he couldn't remember the route.

* * * *

Nurse: Doctor, the Invisible Man is in the waiting room.
M.D.: Tell him I can't see him now.

* * * *

Patient: Doc, I'm afraid I'm going to die.
Doc: Don't worry. That's the last thing you'll do!

* * * *

On his way to his weekly golf game at one of Long Island's most prestigious country clubs, a money grubbing old geezer named Philby happened to catch sight of a teenage caddy idly teeing up balls on the deserted first tee and, with the most graceful swing since Arnold Palmer, knocking them one after another right into the cup, hundreds of yards away.

"Good heavens, young man!" Philby sputtered. "Does anyone else know that you can do that?"

"Nah. I keep it to myself."

"Well, listen my friend, I have an idea that will make us both a great deal of money," said the ever greedy Philby as he winked at the caddy.

The scheme was to set up a match between the club's seasoned golf pro and the callow young caddy and Philby bet heavily on the caddy at 10 to 1.

The day of the big match, however, the kid was terrible. He bogied every hole and wound up with a score of 160.

Philby was enraged. "See here, what do you mean making such a chump out of me? Besides the humiliation, at 10 to 1, I've lost over a hundred thousand dollars!"

"Calm down, Bud," whispered the caddy elbowing the geezer in the ribs. "Next week we'll get a hundred to 1!"

*   *   *   *

Thoughts from the Throne

"Did you ever hear someone say this; 'It was more fun than a barrel of monkeys?' Did you ever smell a barrel of monkeys?"
—Steve Bluestein

"Hey, buddy. How do I get to the Emergency Room?"

"Well, go around the corner, up three stoplights, turn left and pull over to the right. There's a guy on the corner selling hot pretzels. His name is Stosh—just tell him that his sister looks like a dog!"

If Laughter is the Best Medicine, Here are a Couple of Real Pills . . .

A guy goes to a psychiatrist and the doctor says to him, "I see you're an auto mechanic."

"Wow! You're good, Doc. Not a word out of my mouth and you already know what I do for a living!"

"It's just years of training and experience," the shrink replies modestly. "Plus the fact that you're laying UNDER the couch.

❊ ❊ ❊ ❊

Patient: Doc, I sure hope I'm sick.
Doctor: Why on earth would you wish that?
Patient: Because I'd hate to be well and feel like this!

❊ ❊ ❊ ❊

And take a moment to consider the age old question: How many doctors does it take to screw in a light bulb?

The answer? Depends on how much health insurance the light bulb carries.

❊ ❊ ❊ ❊

A woman called the emergency room in a tizzy. "My husband's just swallowed a mouse! What'll I do?"

"Calm down," said the M.D. "Wave a piece of cheese in front of his mouth until I get there."

Ten minutes later, the doctor rushed into the bedroom to find the woman waving a sardine in front of her husband's mouth.

"I told you a piece of cheese, not a sardine!" snapped the doctor.

"I know. I was using cheese but when the mouse stuck its head out, the cat jumped in!"

AGE OLD JOKES

Aging is one of the few things that we all have in common—with the possible exception of Dick Clark—so take some of the time that you've got left and enjoy the following old chestnuts. As Red Skelton's mother once said to him, "Don't take life too seriously. You'll never get out of it alive!"

The top Ten Signs that you're getting up there . . .

10. Your back goes out more than you do.
 9. Before lighting the candles at your birthday party, you have to hand out protective eyewear to the guests . . .
 8. You remember the days when the water was clean and sex was dirty.
 7. The bank mails you the new calendar one month at a time.
 6. Your number is retired by the Social Security Administration.
 5. You have long gray hair down your back. None on your head, just down your back.
 4. You move to a new neighborhood and the local undertaker sends over the welcome wagon.
 3. When you go to the beach you have to fight off little kids trying to play connect-the-dots with your liver spots.
 2. You decide to leave your body to science but science contests the will.
 1. You forgot what number 10 was already.

＊　＊　＊　＊

Three old guys a-rockin' on the front porch: The first geezer says, "Hey, isn't that a '38 Packard?" The second geezer replies, "Nah, it's a '29 Hupmobile." A week passes and the third geezer pipes up, "Well, if you two guys are going to argue all the time, I'm going inside!"

"What's the worst thing about getting old, Dad?" Well, Son, I'll tell you—split hair." "Split hair, huh?" "Yep. Mine split about 10 years ago."

* * * *

The old lady just returned from the Organ Bank quite miffed.

"What's the matter?" asked her daughter.

"I went down there with good intentions, offering to fill out an organ donor card."

"What went wrong?"

"After the doctor looked me over I asked them which organ They might be interested in and he asked me if I happened to own a Wurlitzer!"

Harry, the toothbrush salesman, was the greatest salesman in the history of the toothbrush industry, but he was very secretive about his methods.

One day the sales manager, hoping to get a glimpse of Harry's technique so that he could pass it along to the rest of the sales force, followed his star salesman to a busy street corner downtown and prepared to observe Harry's sales pitch.

Harry set up a small table with a display of toothbrushes and paper cups filled with a brownish-green fluid.

As people passed by, Harry snared a likely prospect by saying, "Good morning, sir. We're test marketing a new soft drink called Poopsie Coola. Care to try a sample?"

The man took the paper cup and knocked back a mighty swig of the drink but then spit it out ala Danny Thomas and screamed, "That stuff tastes like motor oil!"

"It is," smiled Harry. "Care to buy a toothbrush?"

* * * *

Did You Hear the One About . . .?

The surgeon who moonlighted as a comedian? He always had everybody in stitches . . .

* * * *

The kid who got so chubby that she had to have her hula-hoop let out?

* * * *

The woman who was so dumb that every time she made chocolate chip cookies, there were M&M shells all over the kitchen floor?

* * * *

The guy who was so bald that instead of a toupee he had to wear a three-pee?

* * * *

The fellow who was so meek that he once spent an entire afternoon at a 4-Way stop?

* * * *

The hypochondriac tree? It's bark is worse than it's blight . .

* * * *

The guy who wanted to spend his vacation water-skiing but gave up in disgust? He couldn't find a lake on a hill.

* * * *

The retired astronaut who opened an unsuccessful restaurant on the moon? The food was great but there just was no atmosphere.

* * * *

The boxer who was so bad that he made most of his money renting advertising space on the soles of his shoes?

* * * *

The newlyweds who spent their honeymoon at a "Friday the 13th" film festival? They really loved each shudder.

* * * *

The strike down at the U.S. Mint? The workers are demanding to make less money.

* * * *

The college football team in which all the players made straight A's in the same semester? Next term they'll work on writing B's.

* * * *

The guy who drove to Atlantic City in a $10,000 car and returned home in a $50,000 vehicle? A brand new bus!

Thoughts from the Throne

"I make stained-glass contact lenses — for people who want to sleep in church."
—London Lee

Years ago on the hit Russian game show "Bowling For Rubles," two contestants, one from Czechoslovakia and the other from Poland, fought to a draw and so were both awarded the first prize, an all expense paid hunting trip in beautiful Siberia.

A few days later, the pair arrived at the hunting camp at the edge of the woods but their guide was sick so they decided to set out on their own in pursuit of the great Russian bear.

After days of tracking a pair of the giant beasts, one male and the other female, they caught up with their quarry. The hunters drew a bead on the bears and fired. It was then that they discovered that the "all-expense paid" hunting trip apparently didn't include ammo.

The clicks of their rifles roused the bears which gave chase and attacked the hunters. The Pole was dazed and fell down the river bank and drifted downstream. Hours later, he came to and made his way back to the camp.

He told the guide his story and a rescue party was organized.

The searchers trekked through the woods for days without finding anything but then, suddenly, there were the two bears once again.

The female bear was still chewing on the hunter's boot when the searchers fired.

The rescuers rushed to the female bear and since it was obvious that they were too late, they grimly set about confirming the fate of the Czechoslovakian hunter. They cut the female open but found nothing and so it dawned on them that this bear's mate must have gotten him. It was at that point the Pole uttered the immortal words, "The Czech's in the male!"